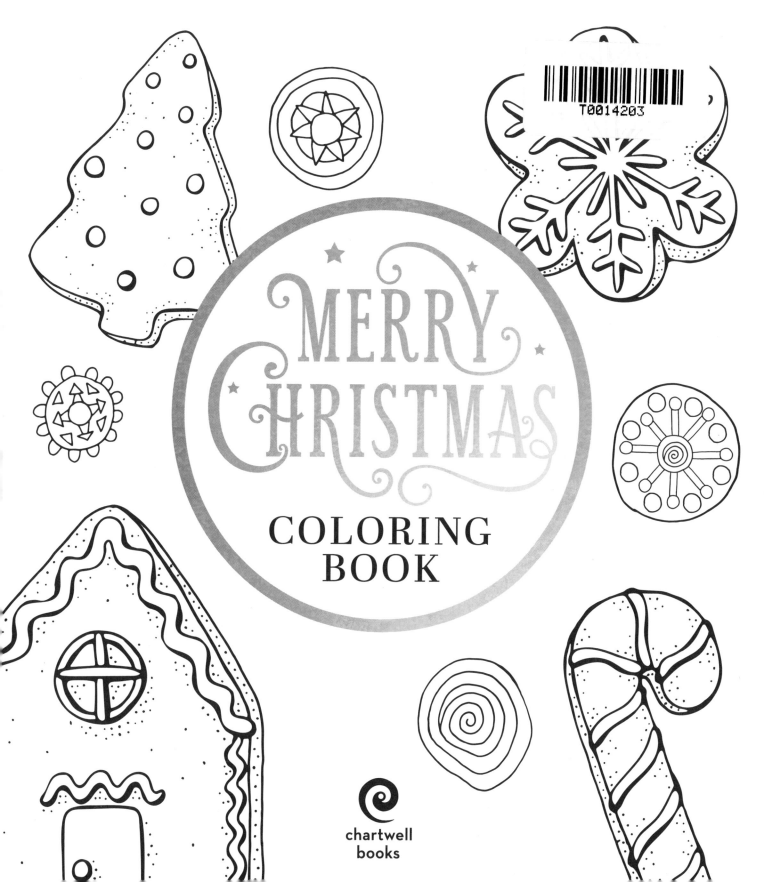

MERRY CHRISTMAS

COLORING BOOK

chartwell
books

'Tis the Season for Coloring!

Celebrate the Christmas season by sitting next to a crackling fire with a cozy blanket and a coloring book!

The holidays are meant to be joyful, but they can also be stressful and overwhelming. Take a break from all the holiday activities like ice skating, baking, and gift wrapping, and relax with the beautiful illustrations in the *Merry Christmas Coloring Book*. Inside you'll find detailed designs of presents, Christmas trees, Santa Claus, and more.

Coloring is a meditative and soothing activity. It requires no artistic experience or skills. It's a fun and low-pressure way to explore your creative side. You can use festive holiday colors like red and green or any other colors you wish. Remember there is no right or wrong way to color these pages. Start coloring today!

Merry Christmas to you!

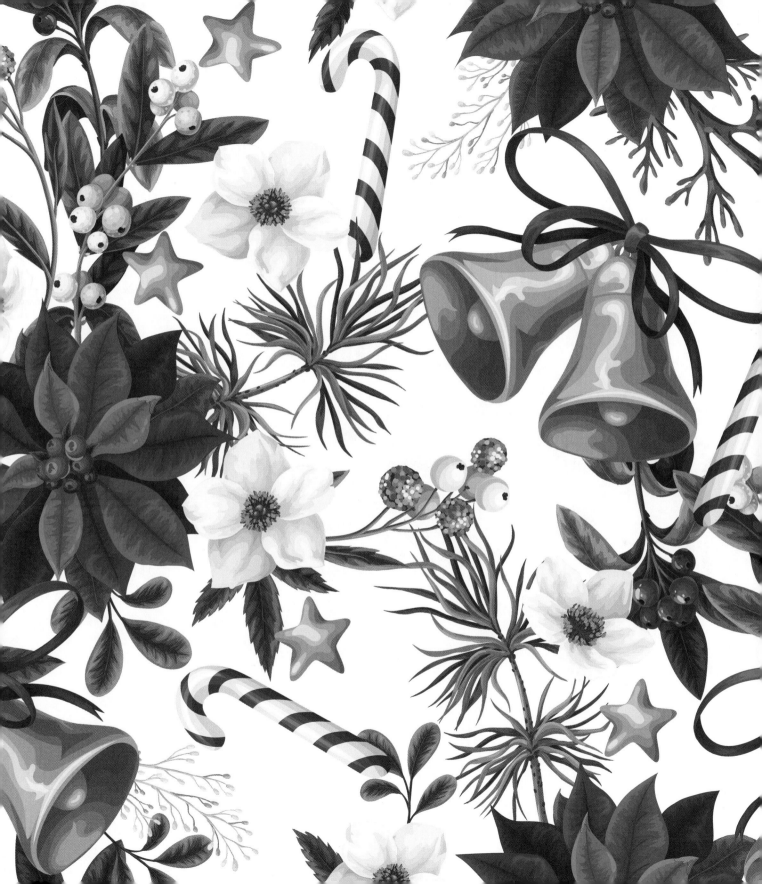

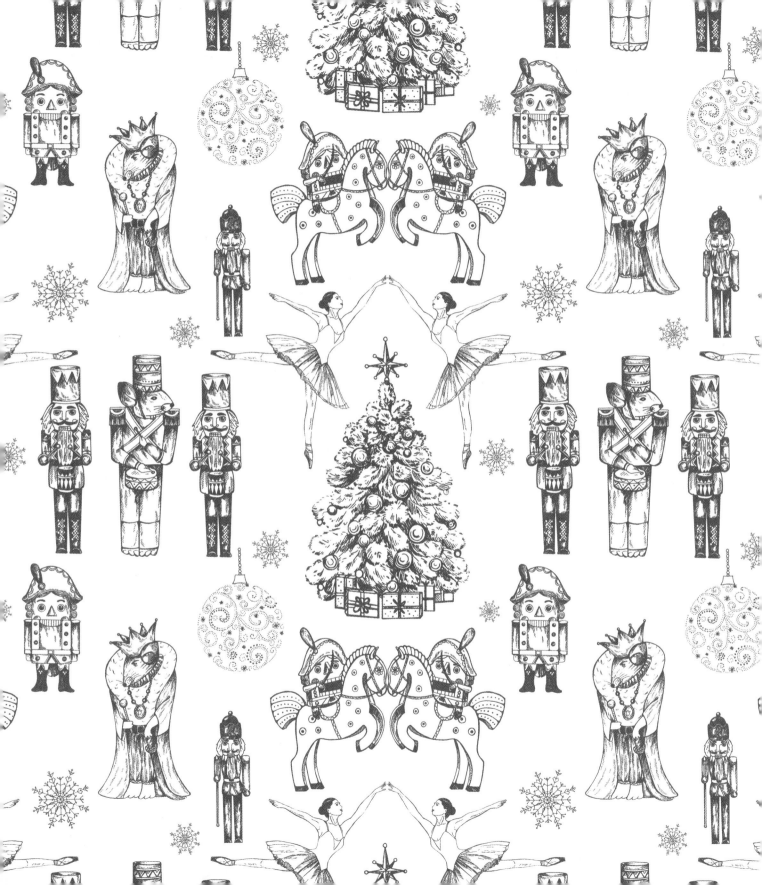

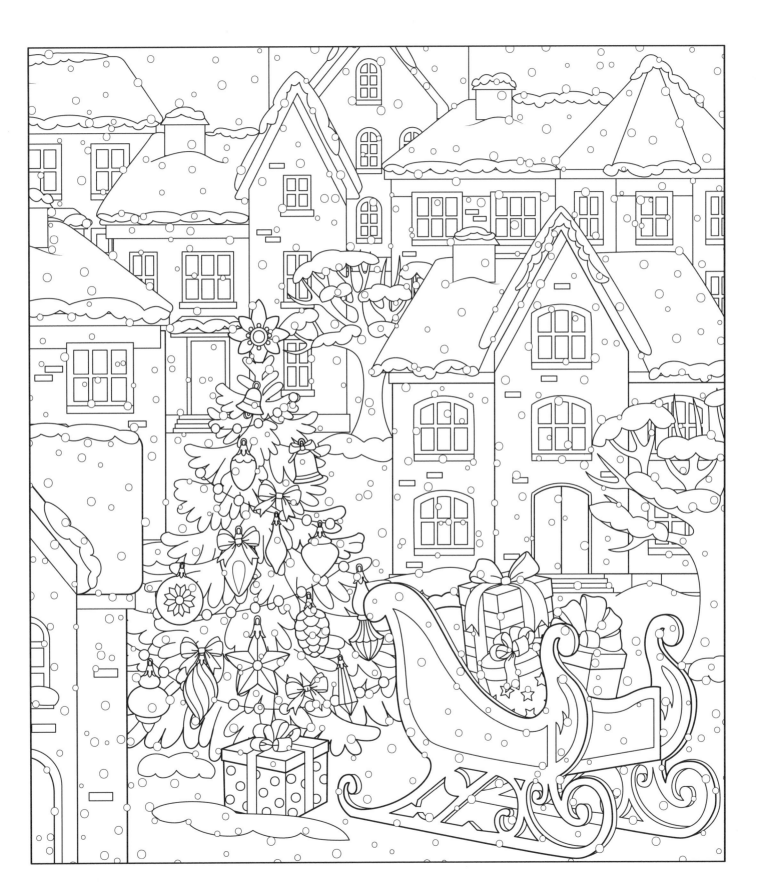

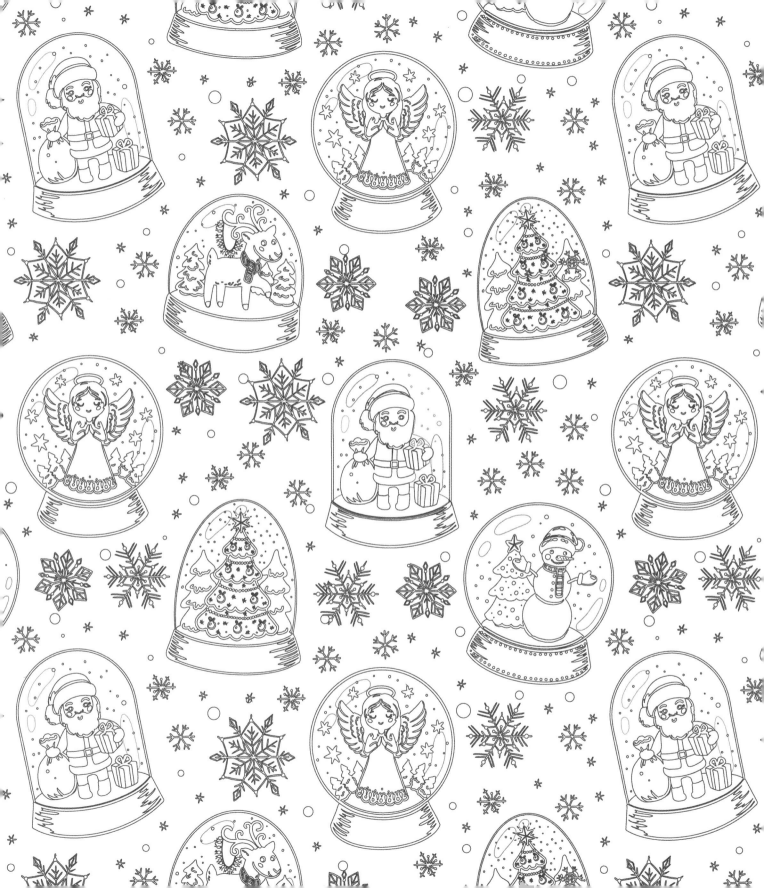

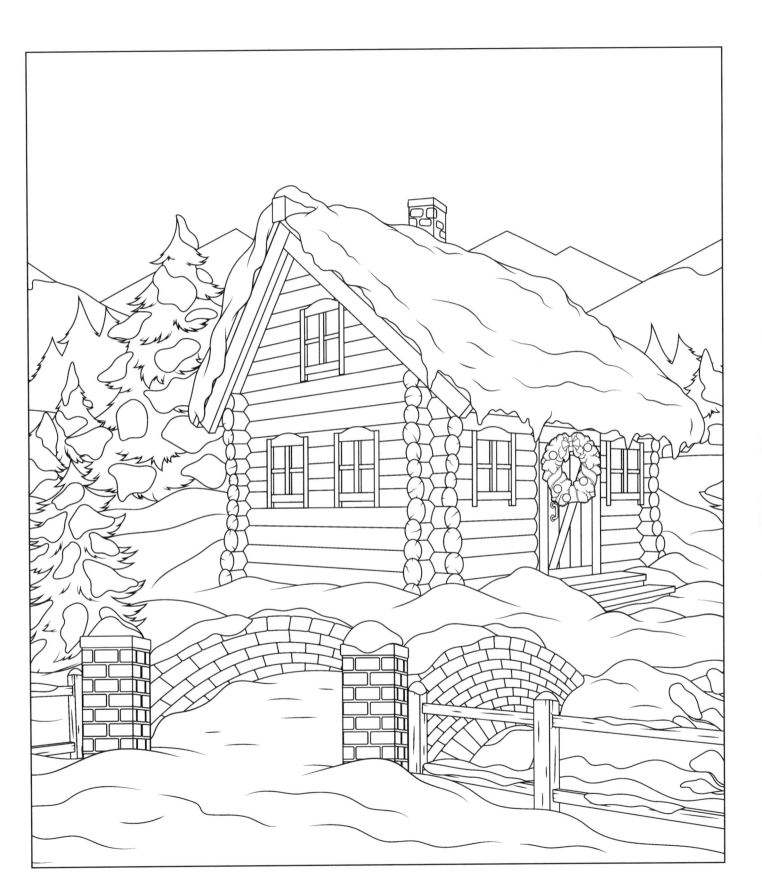

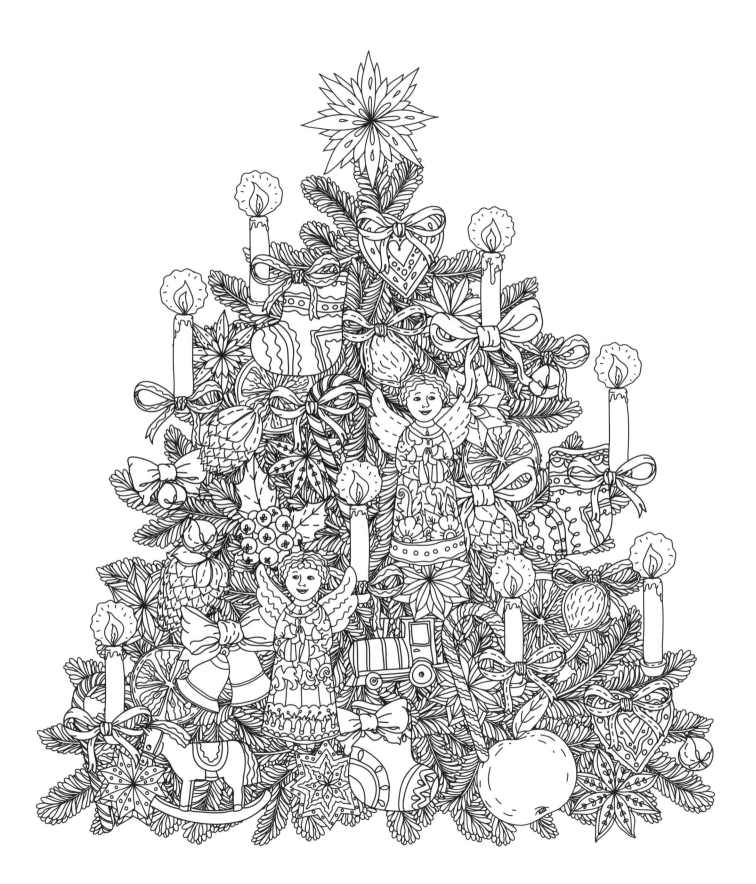

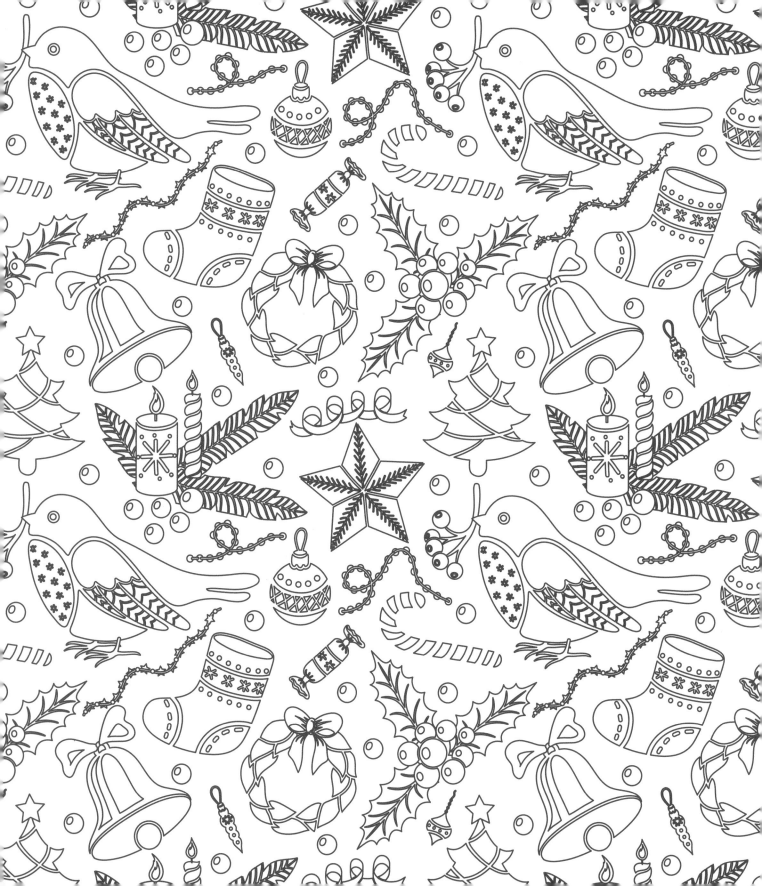

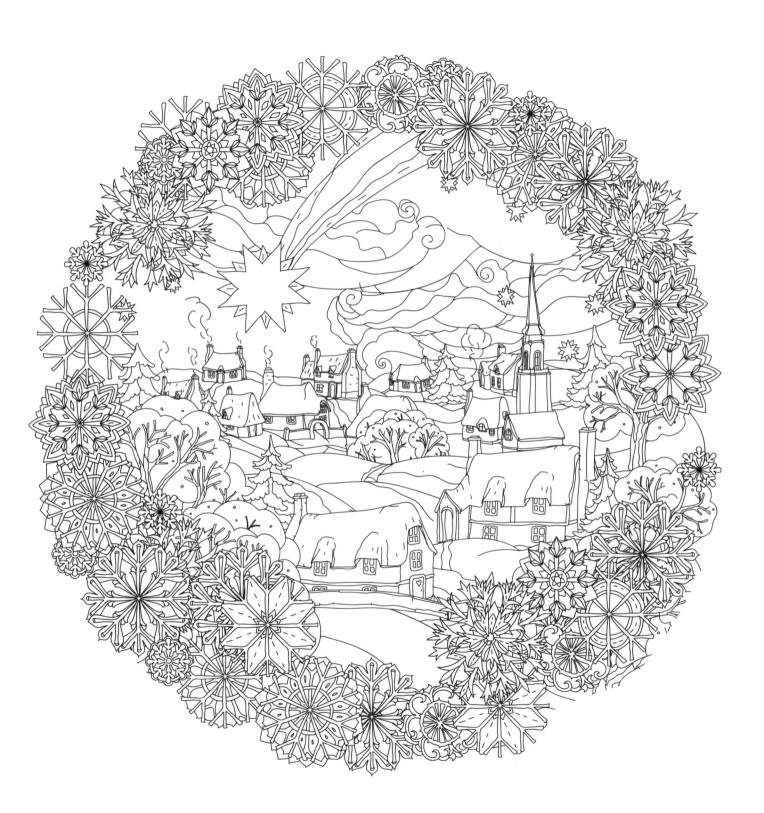

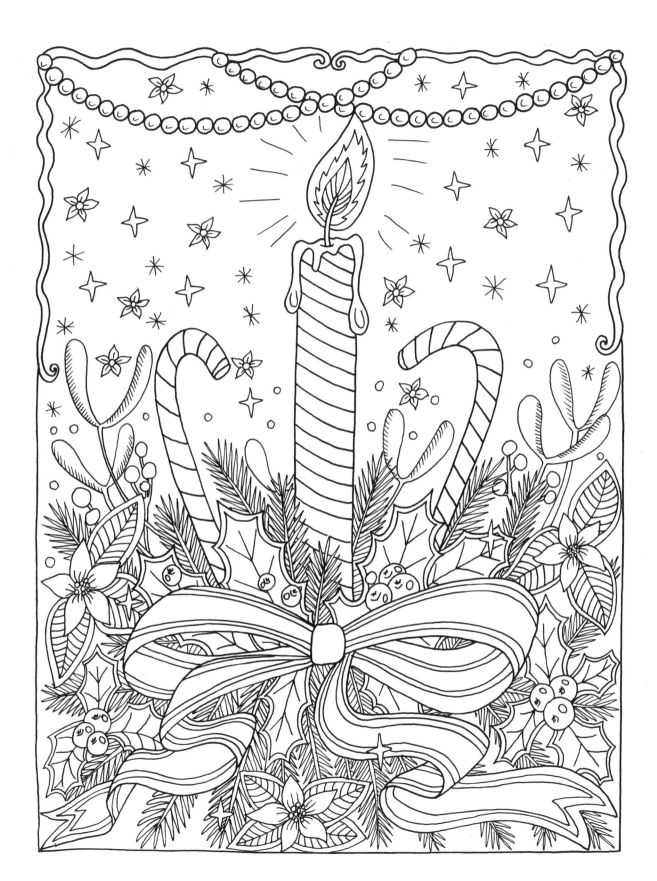

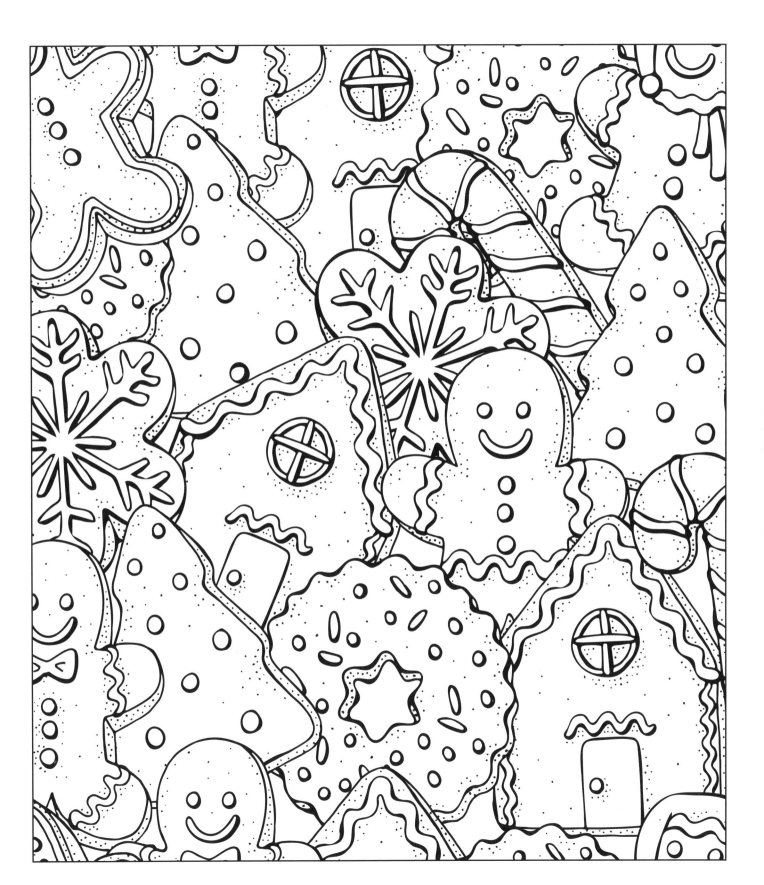

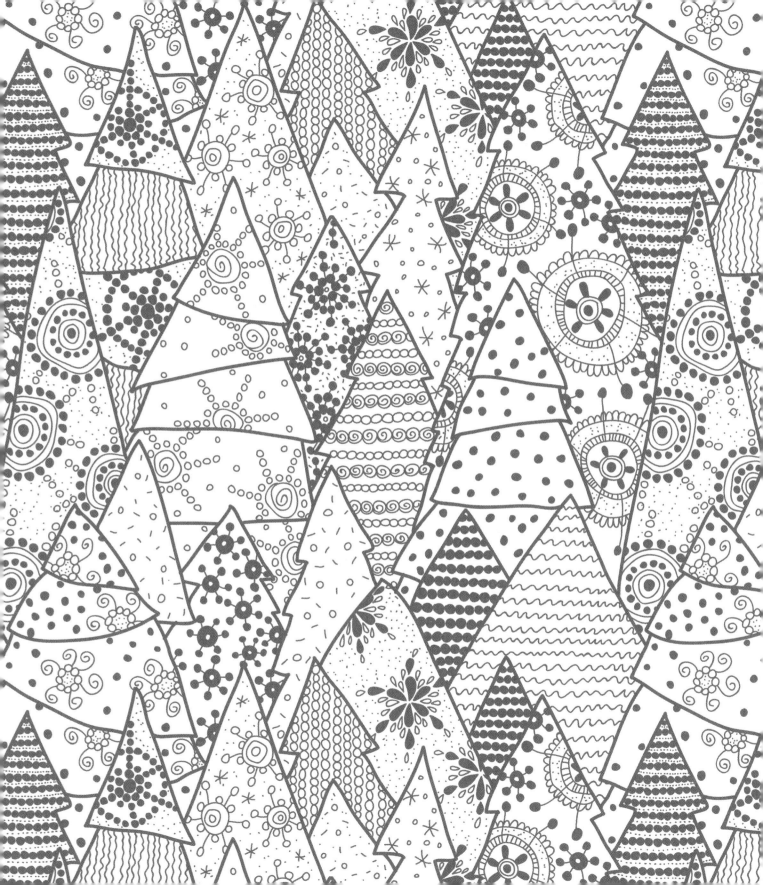

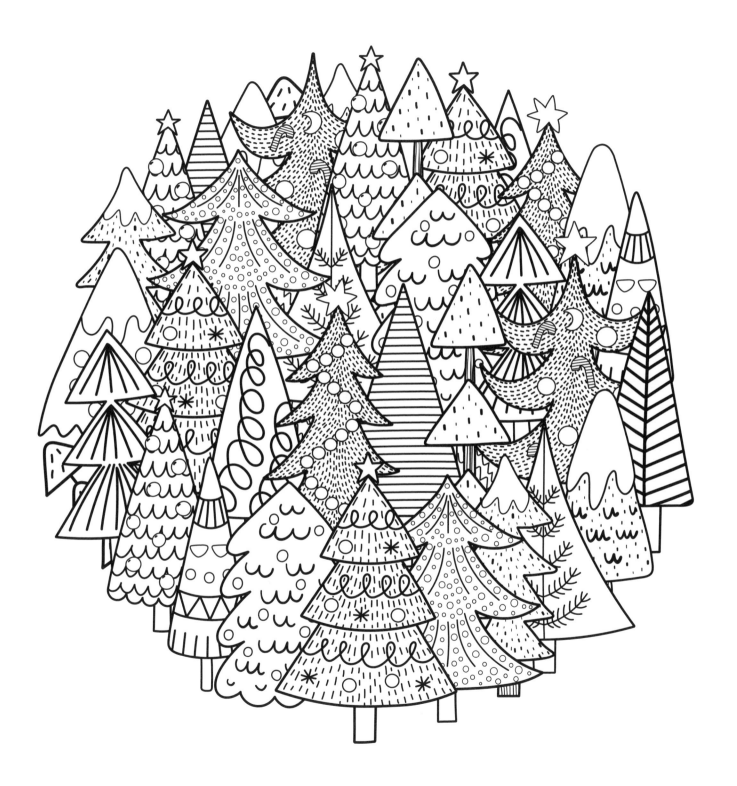

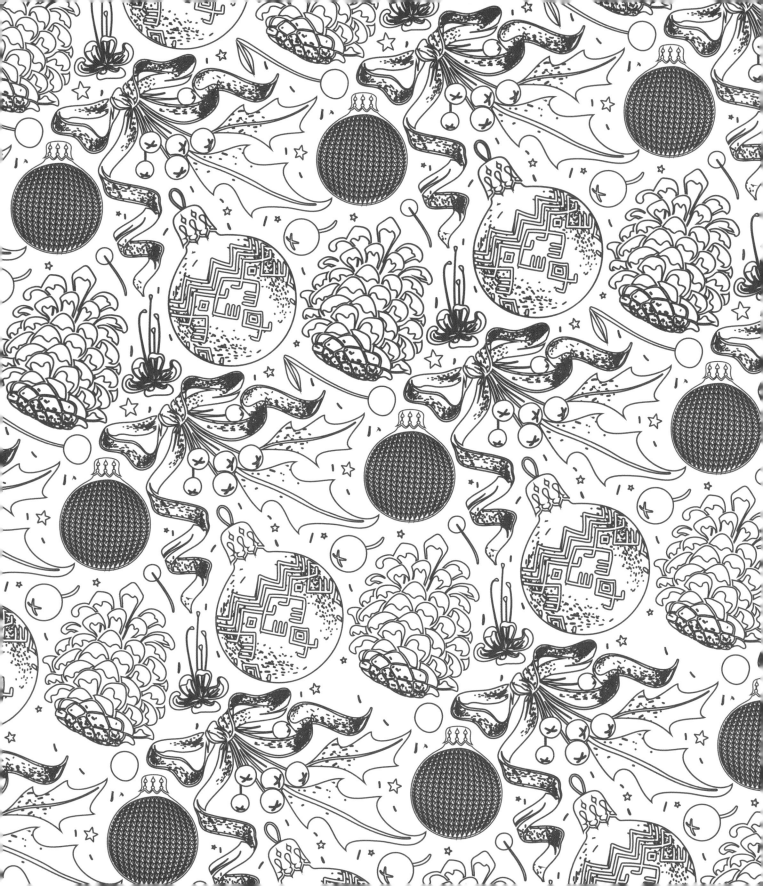

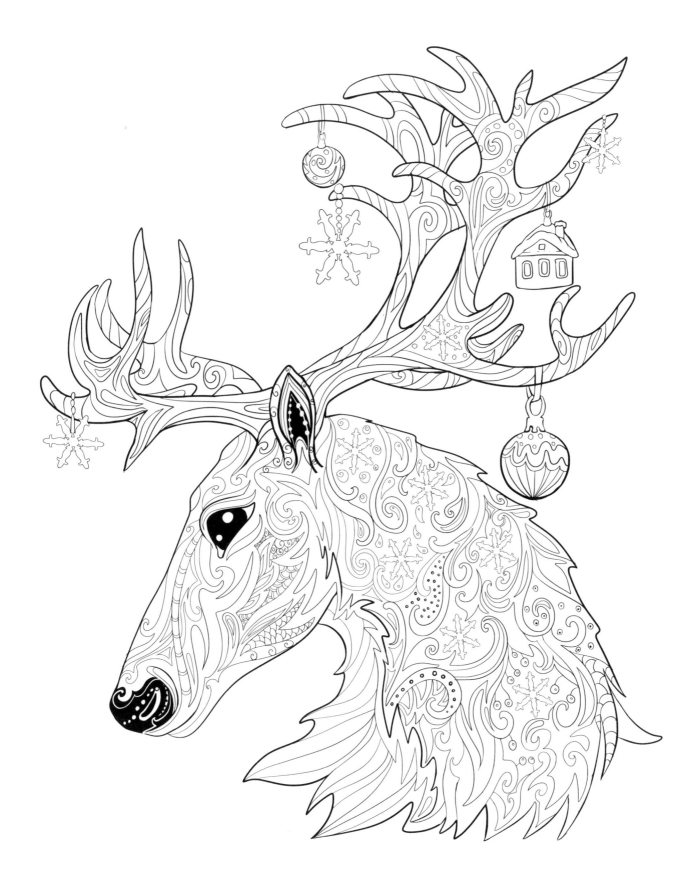

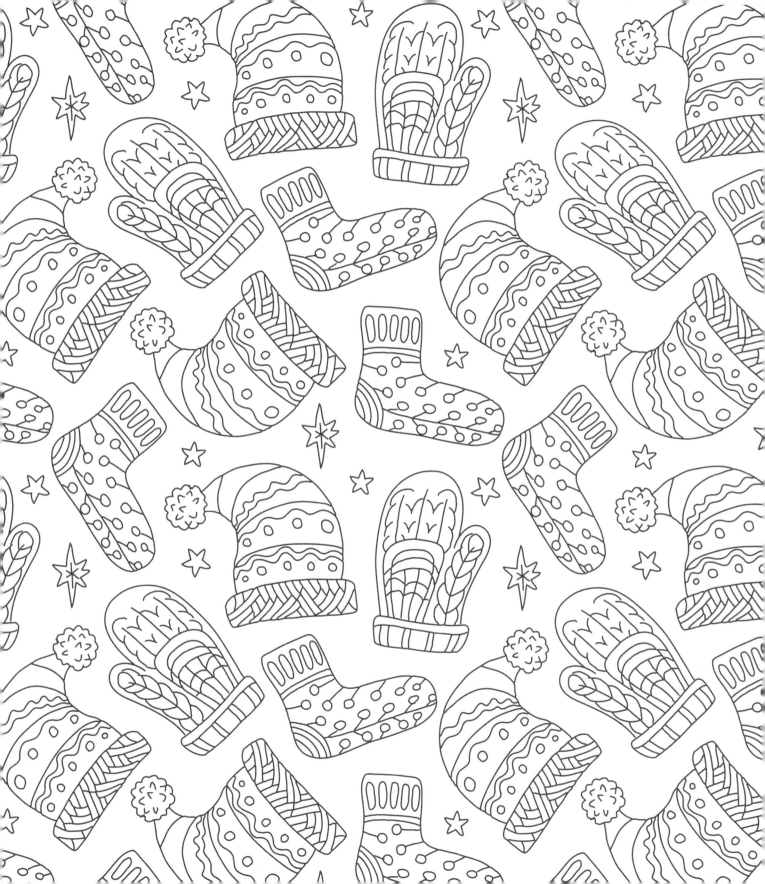

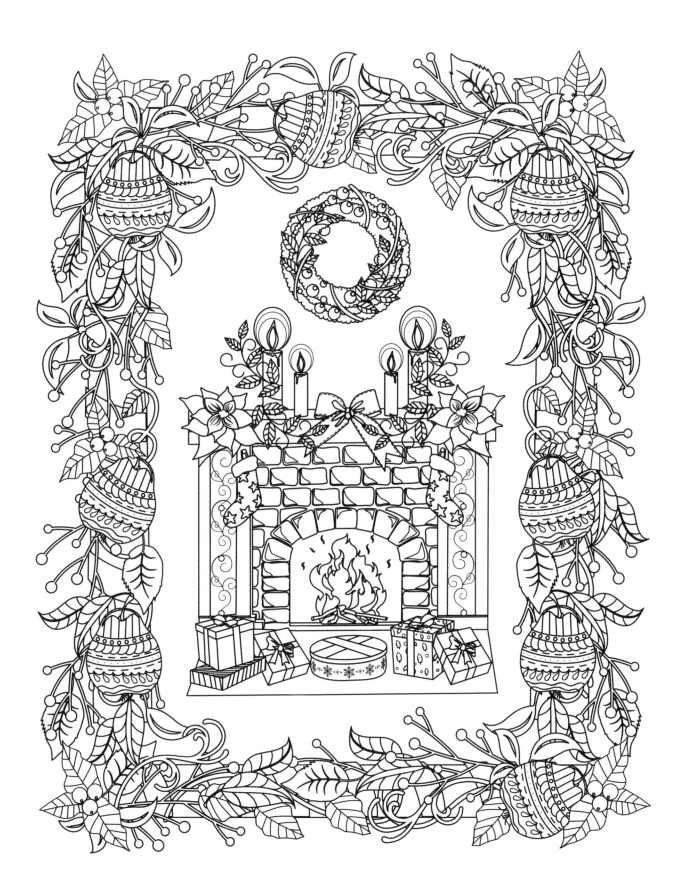

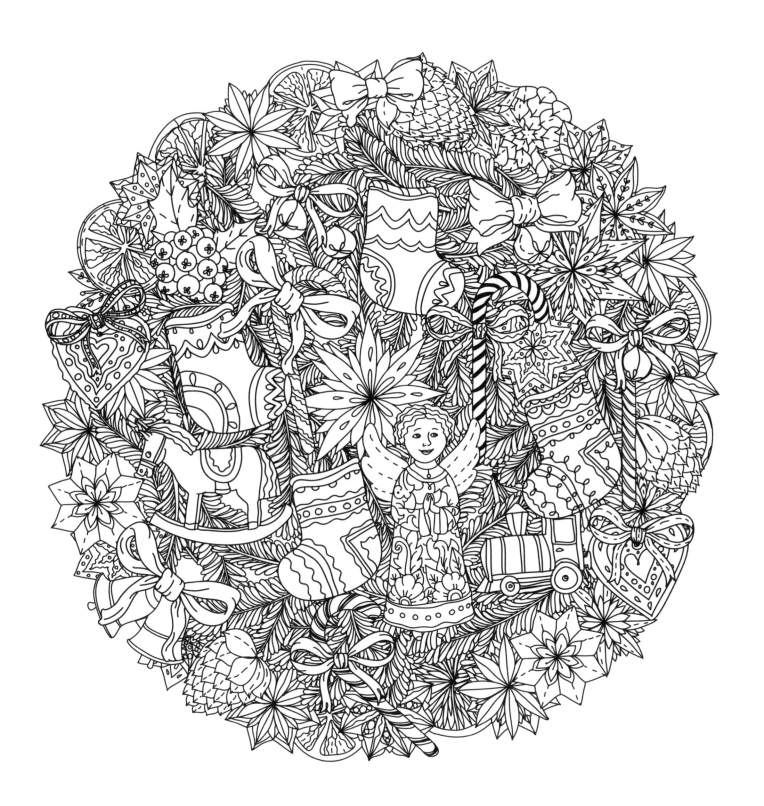

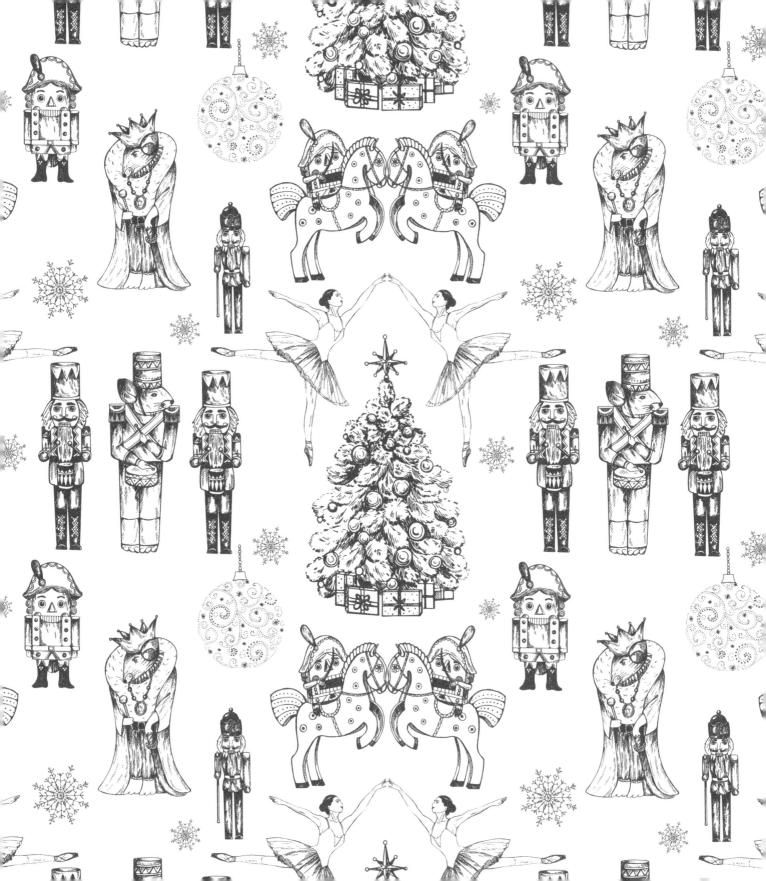

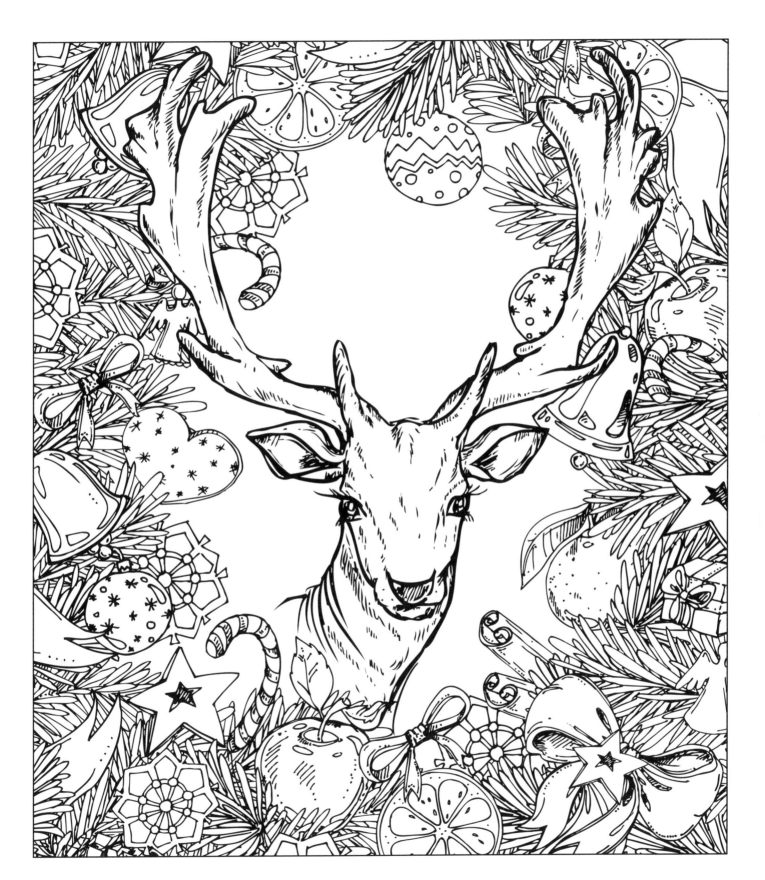

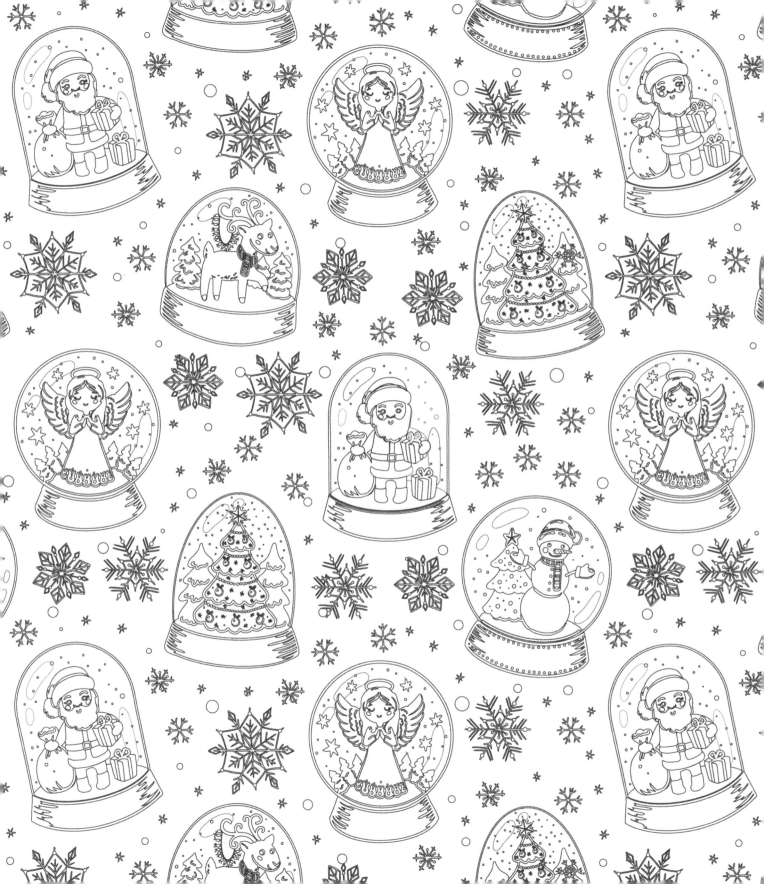

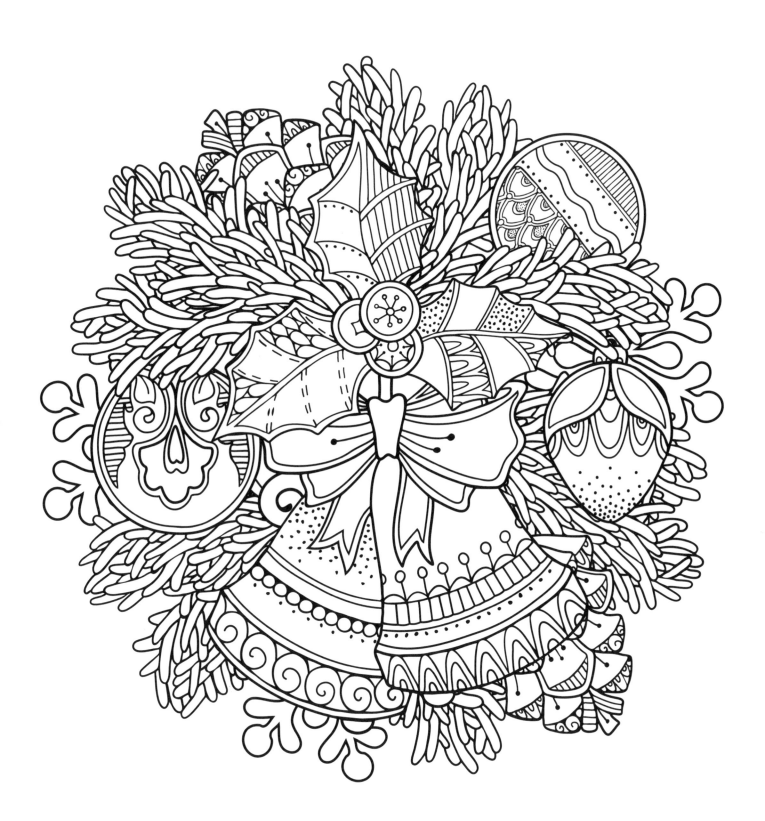

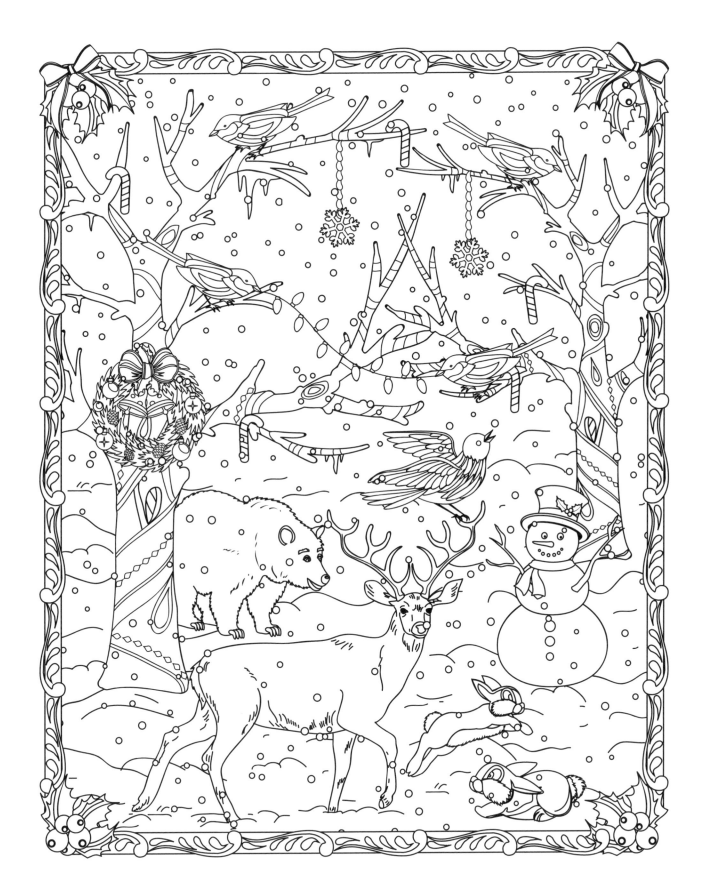

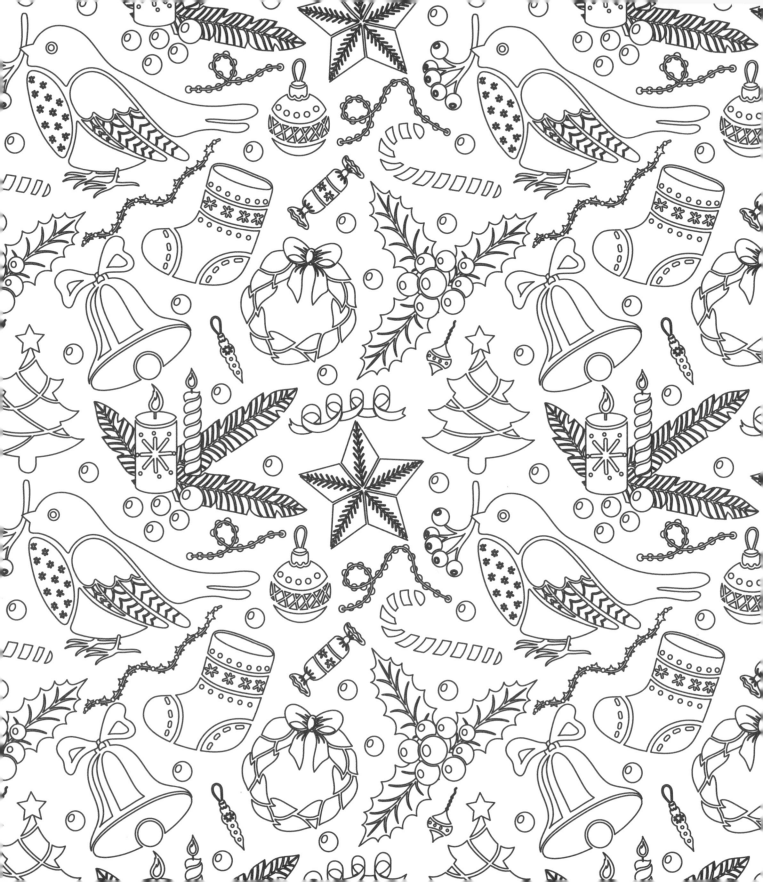

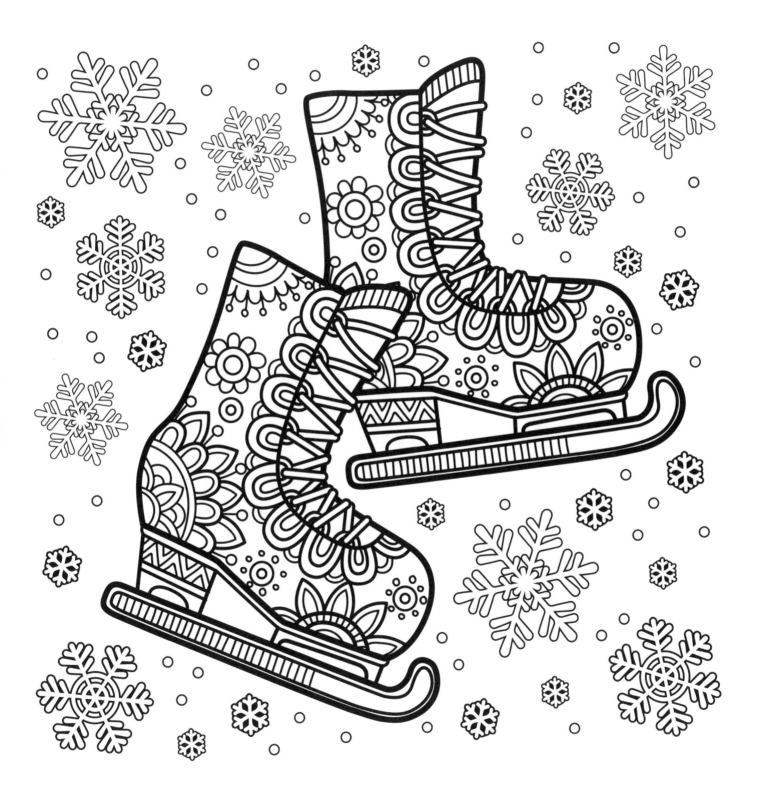

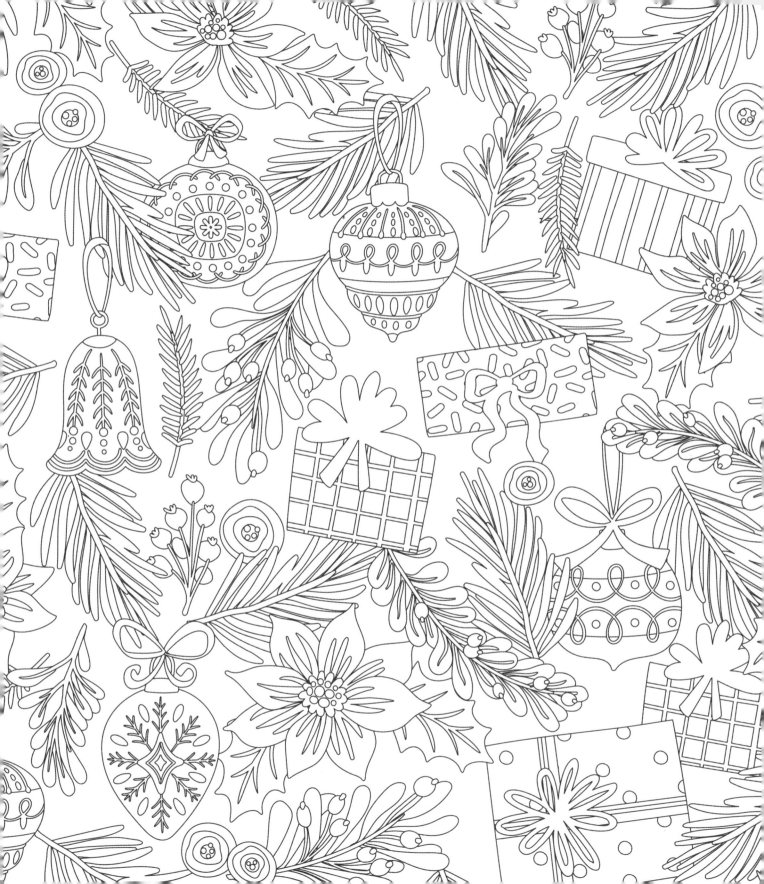

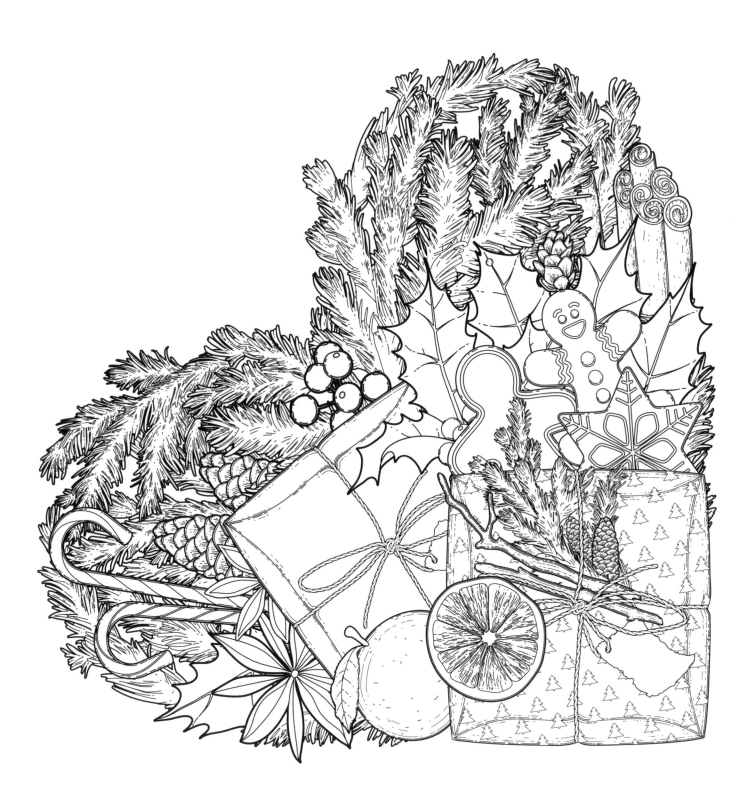

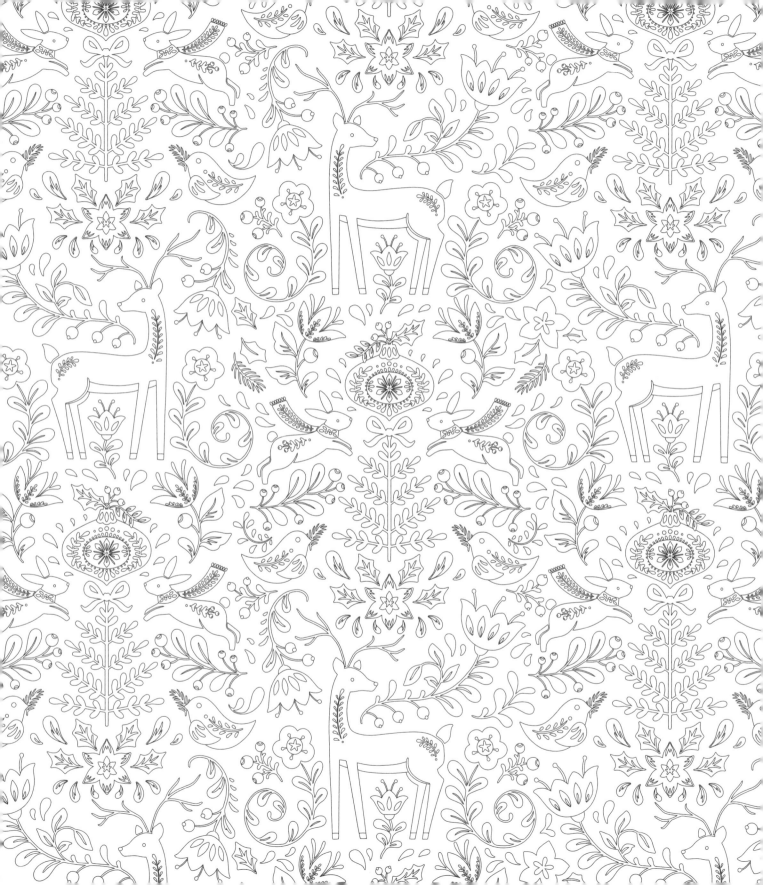

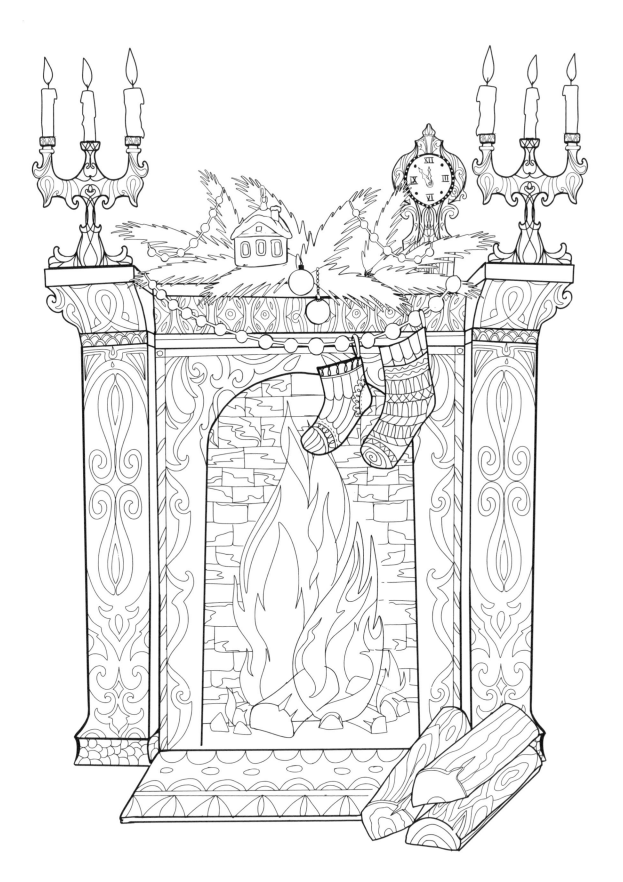

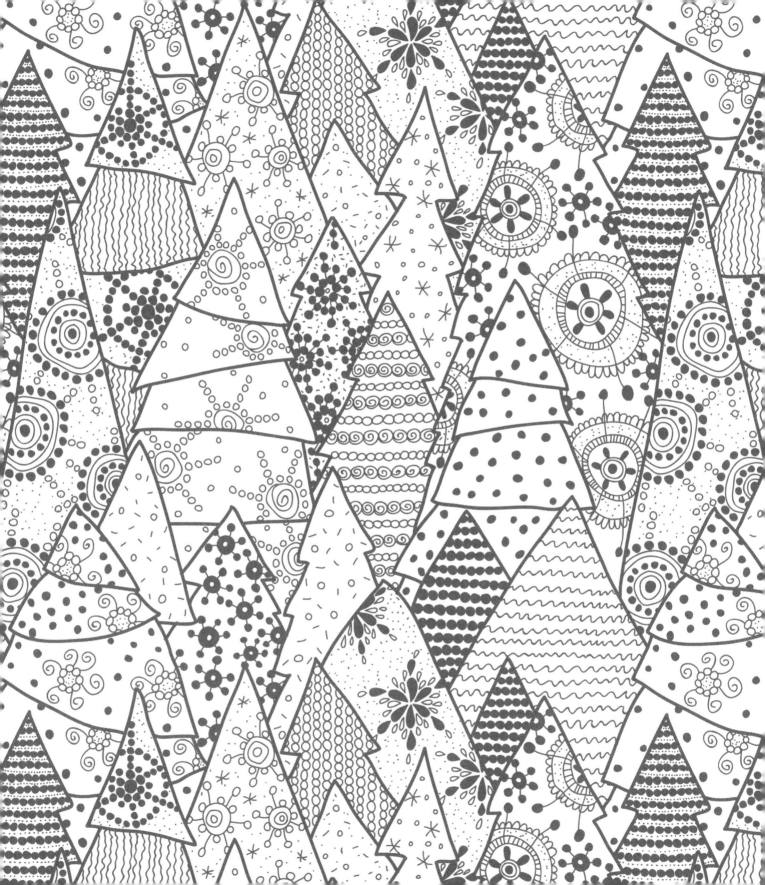

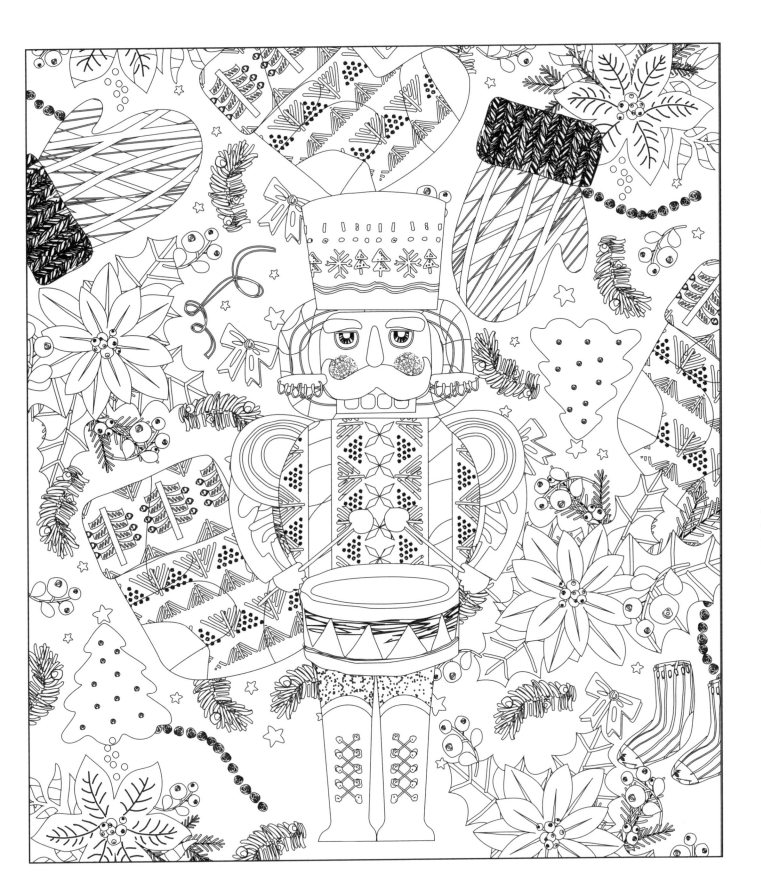

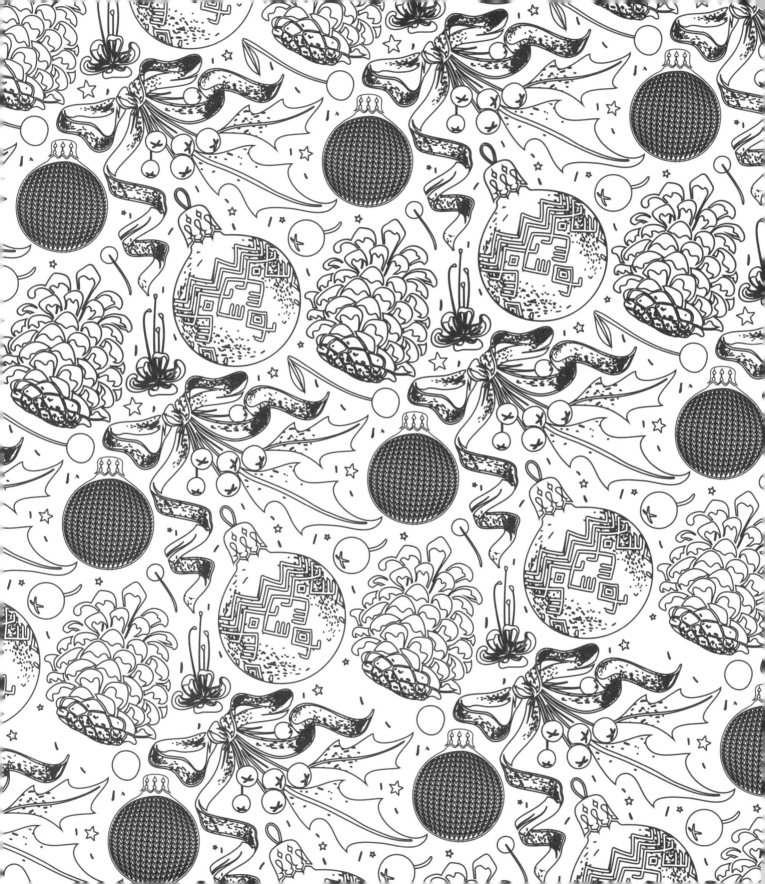

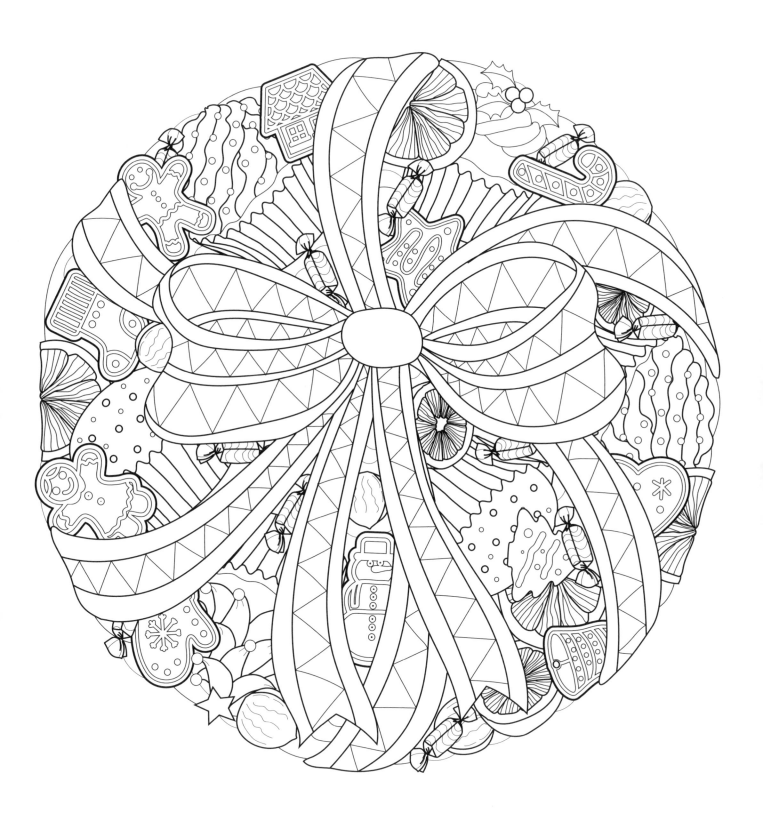

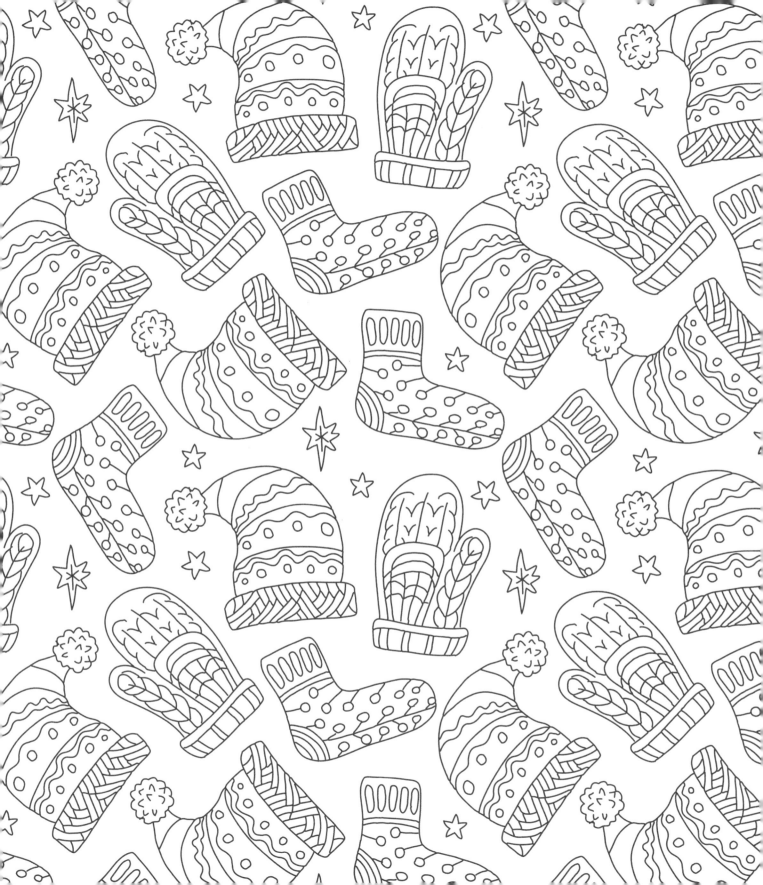

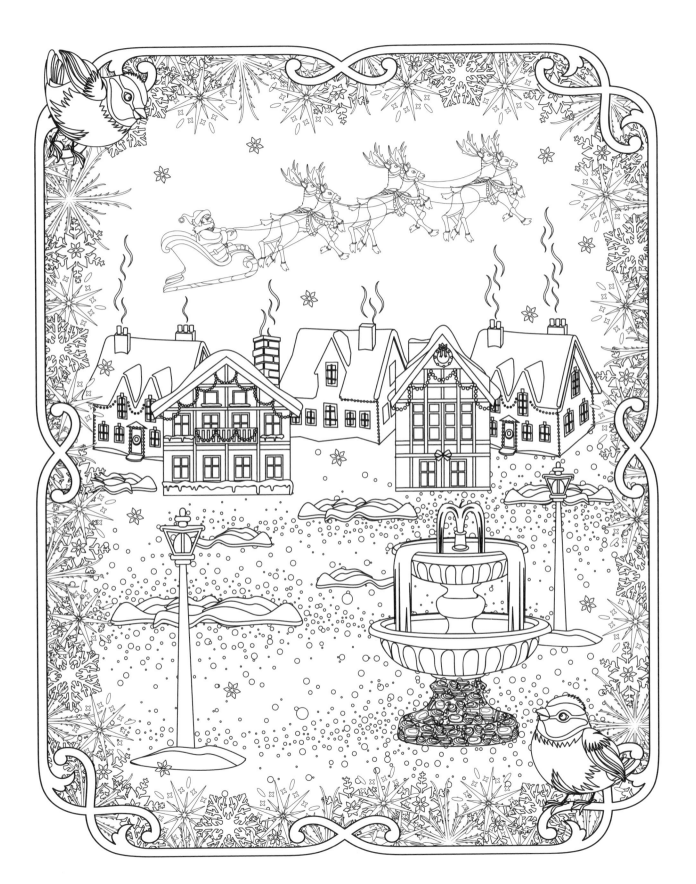

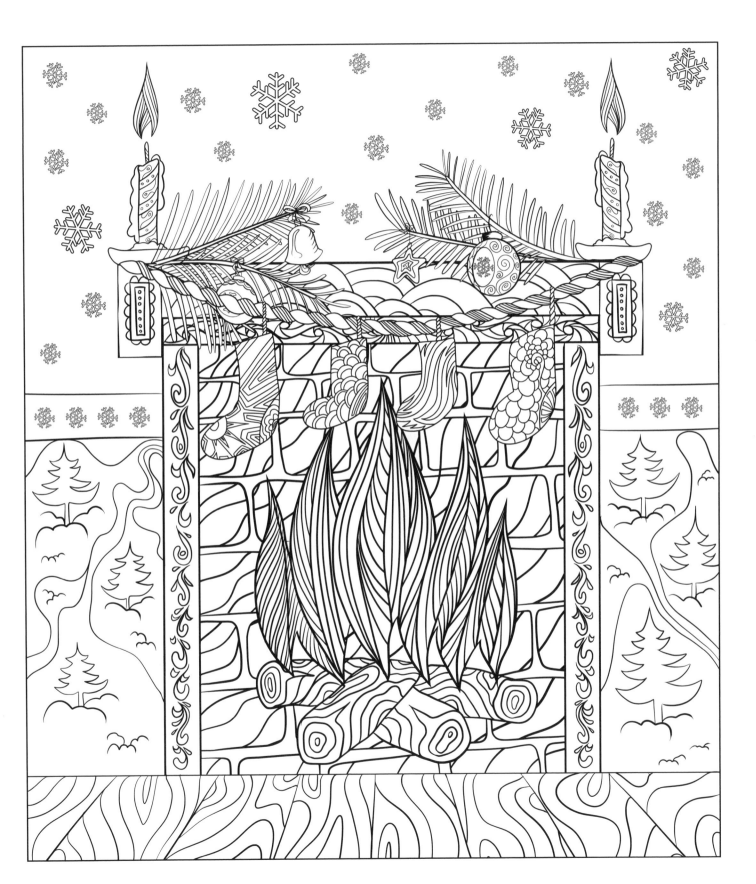

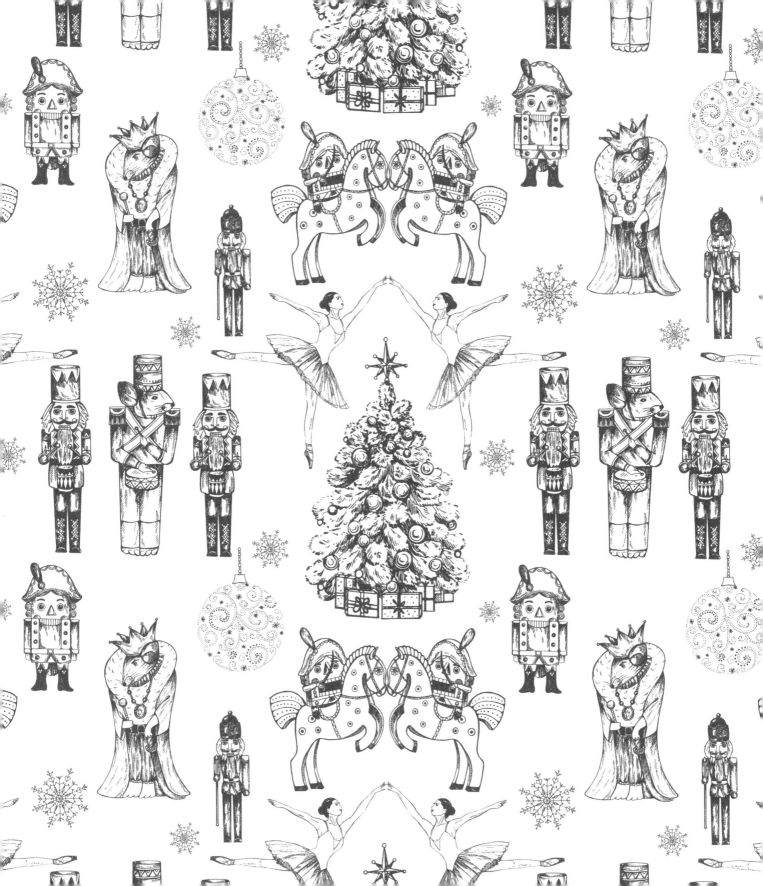

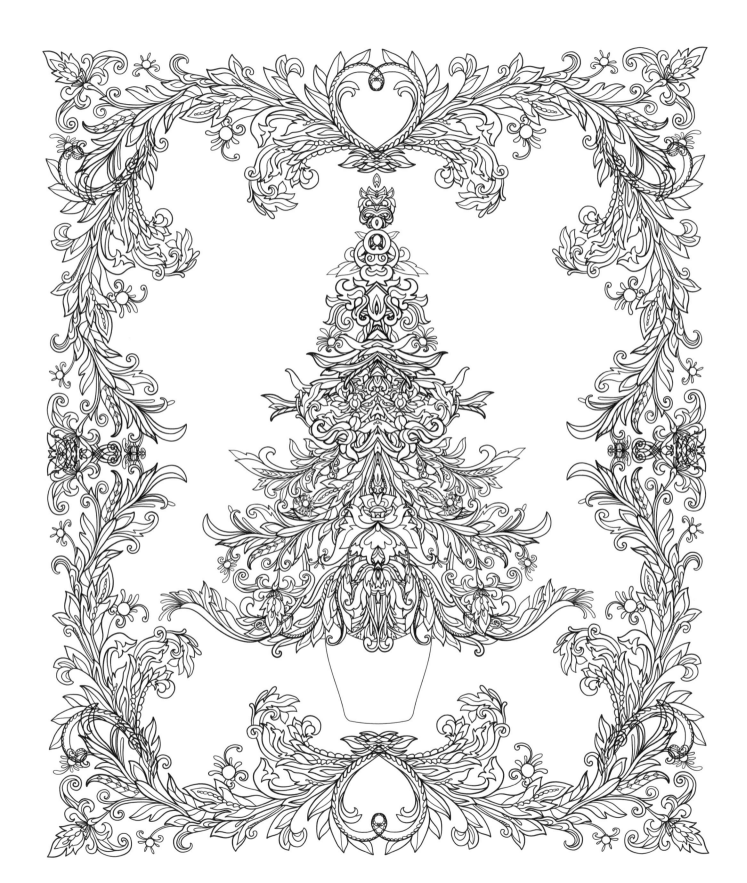

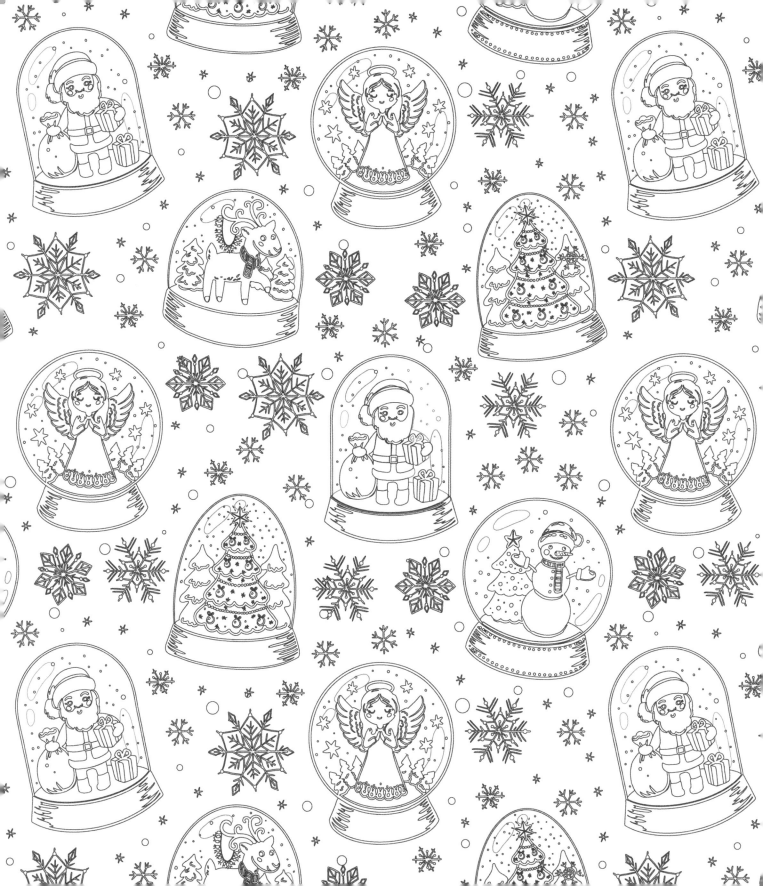

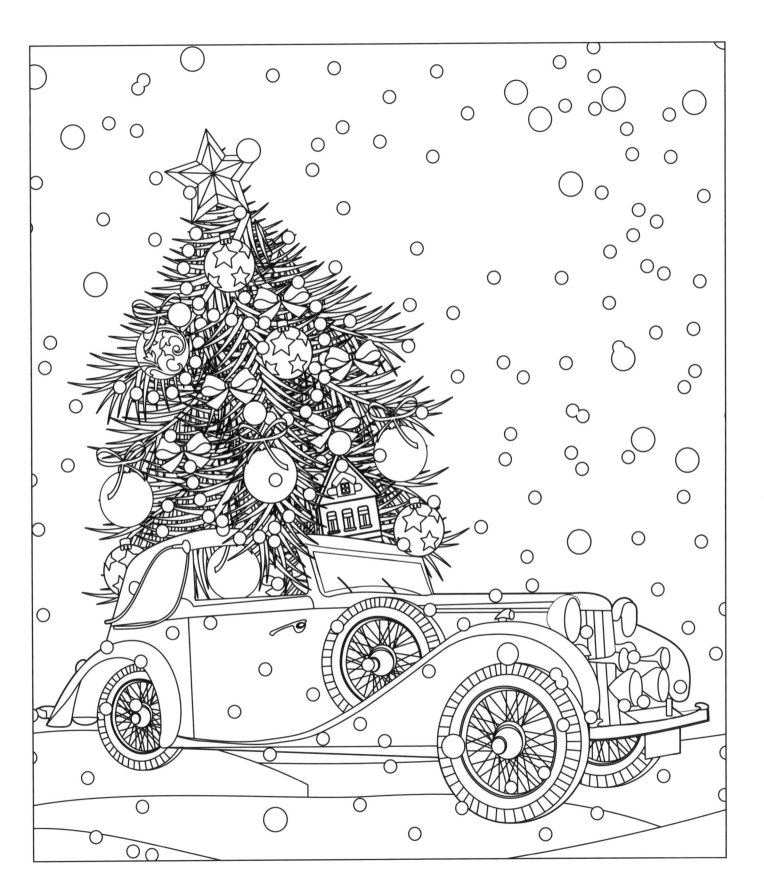

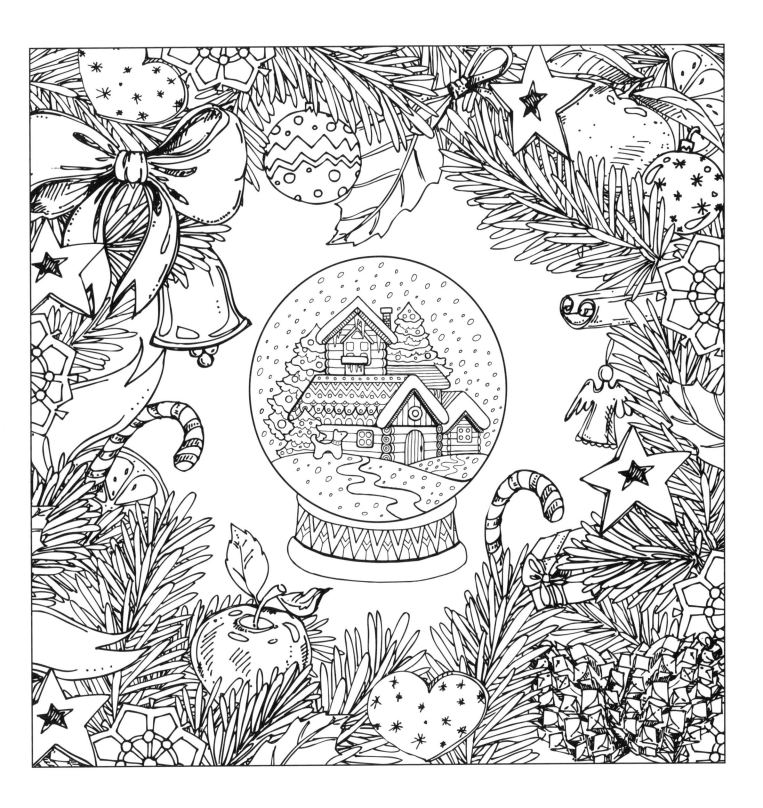

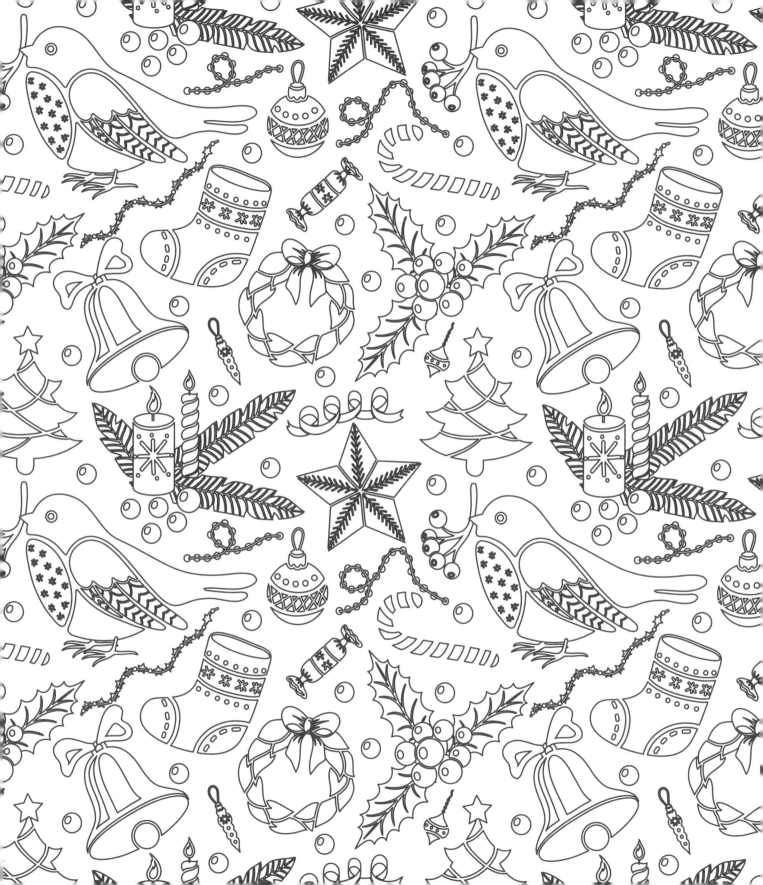

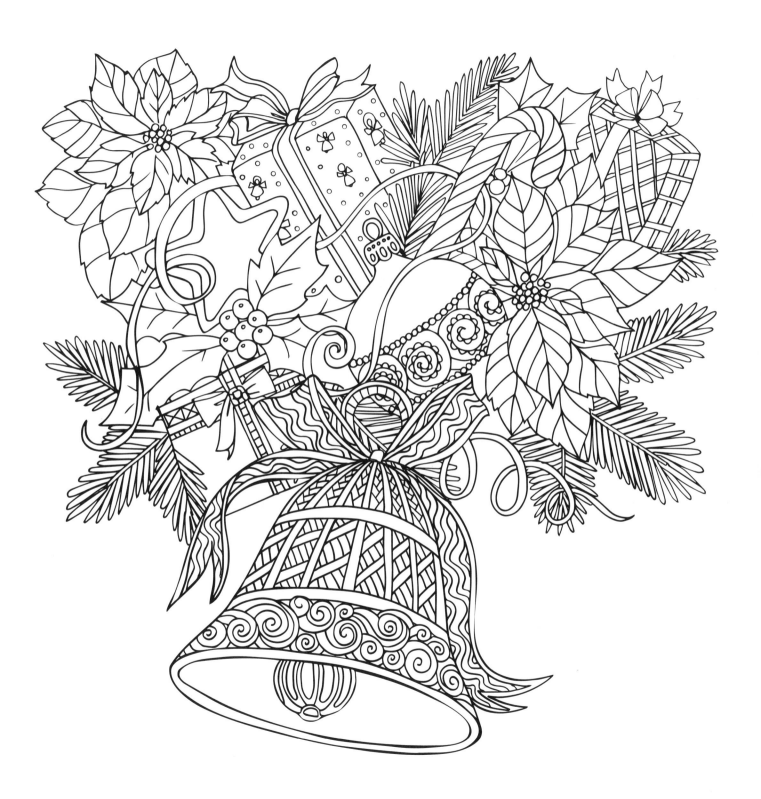

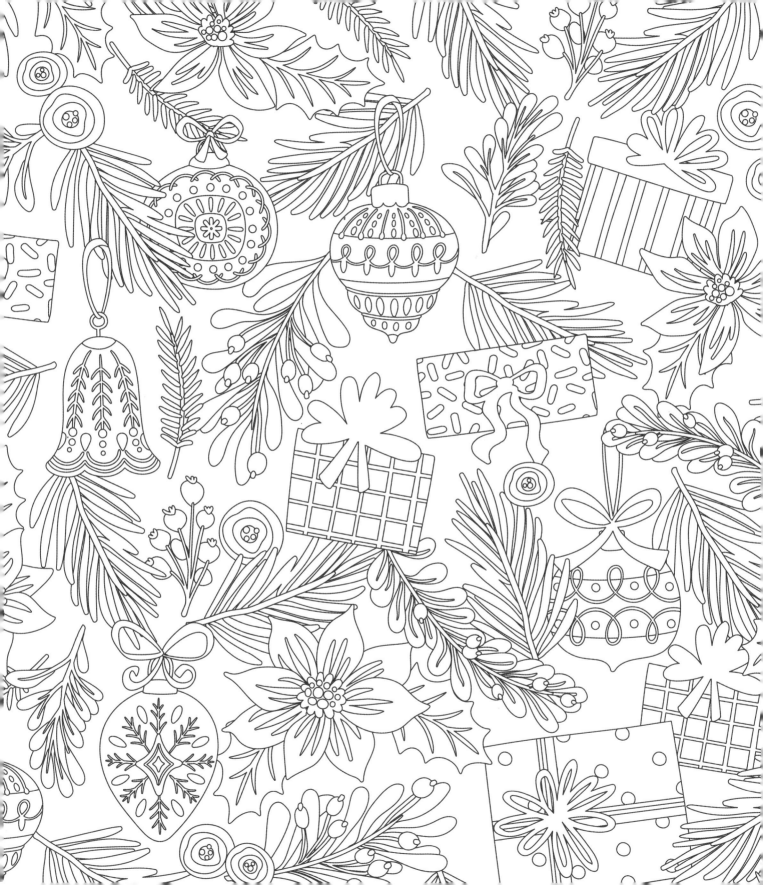

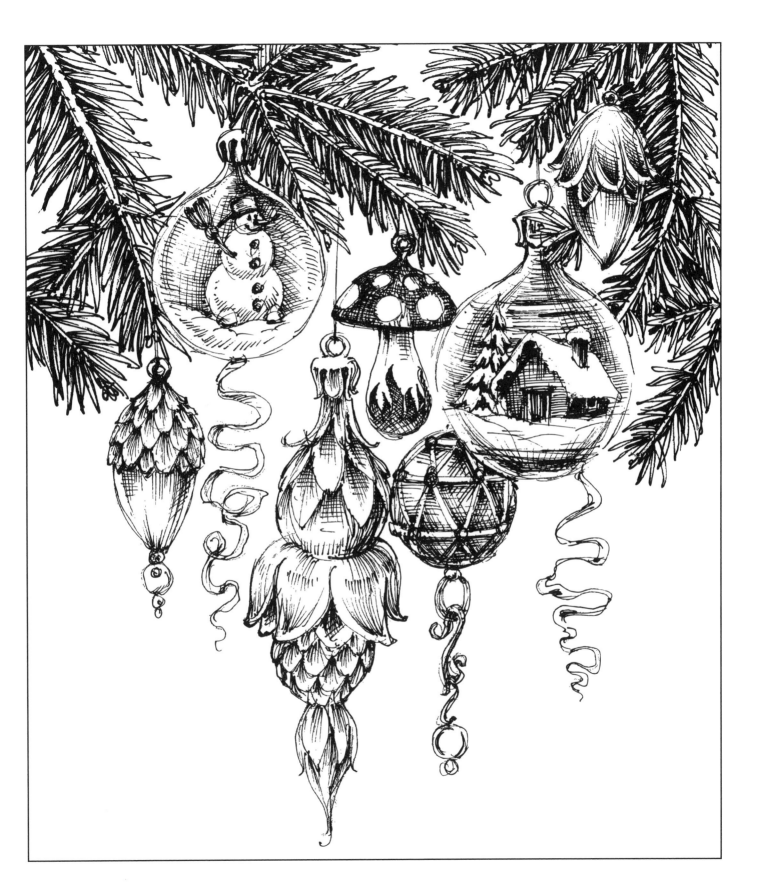

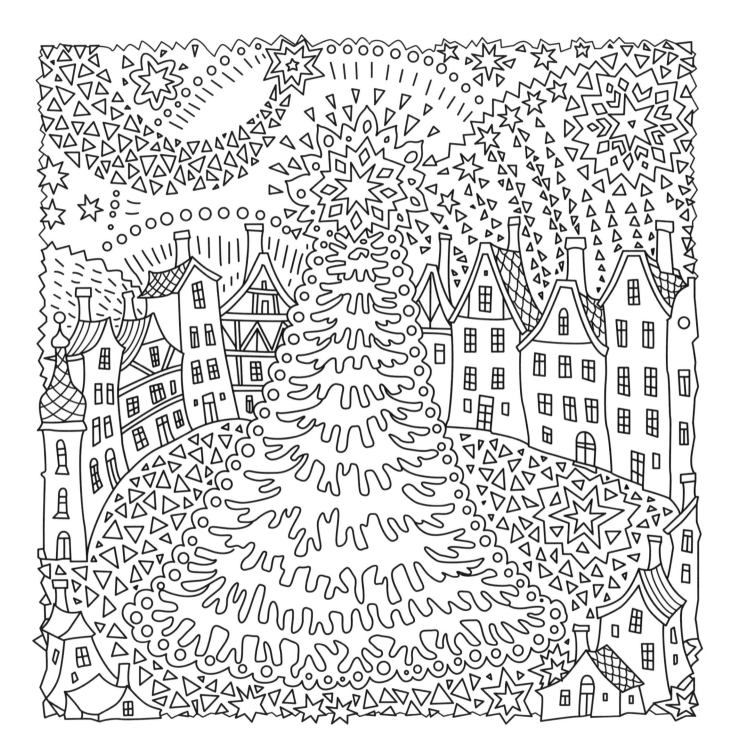

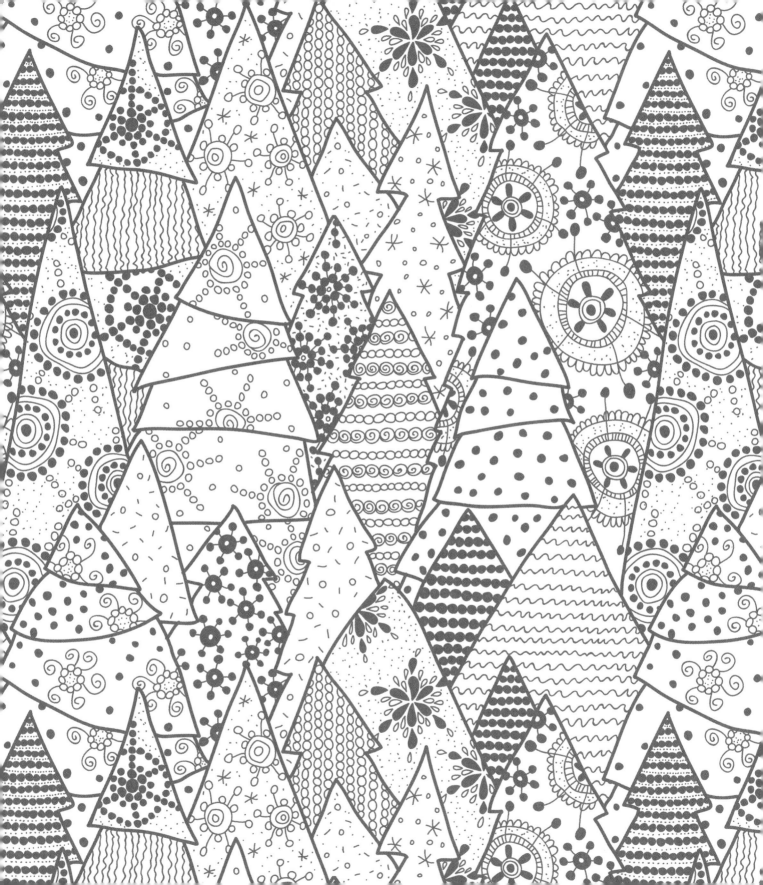

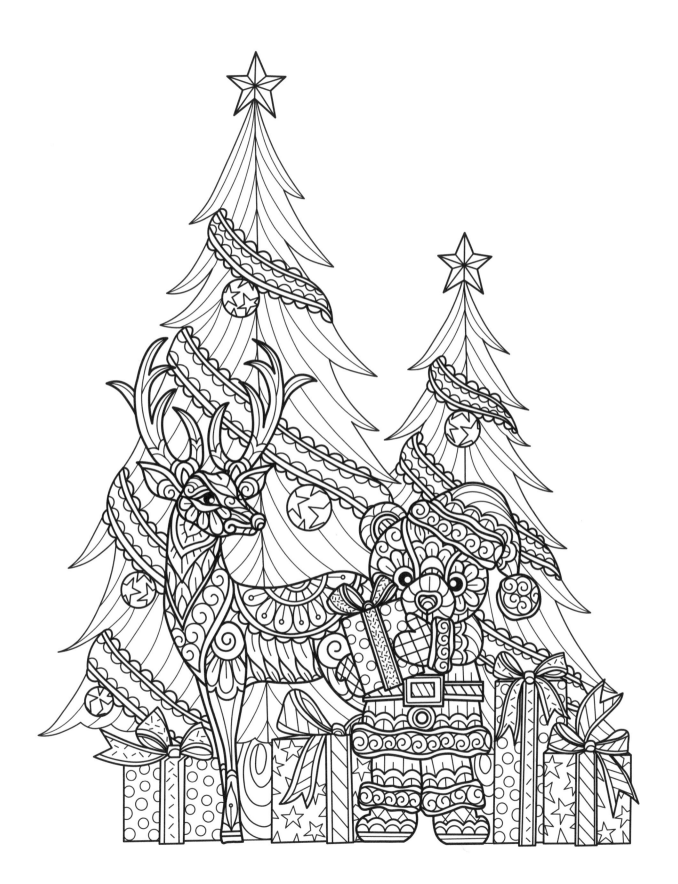

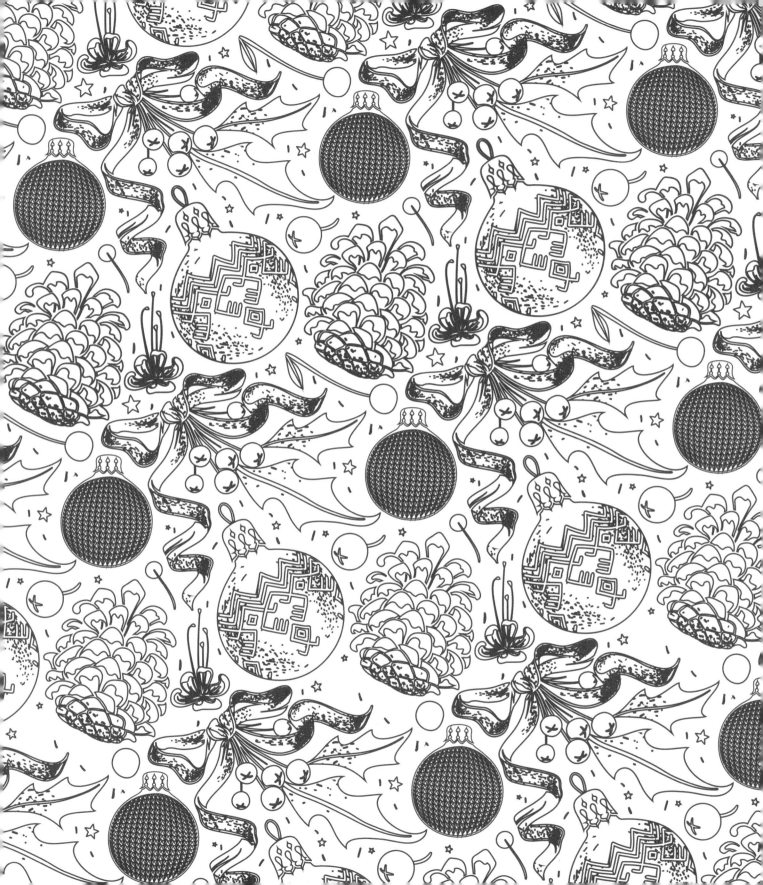

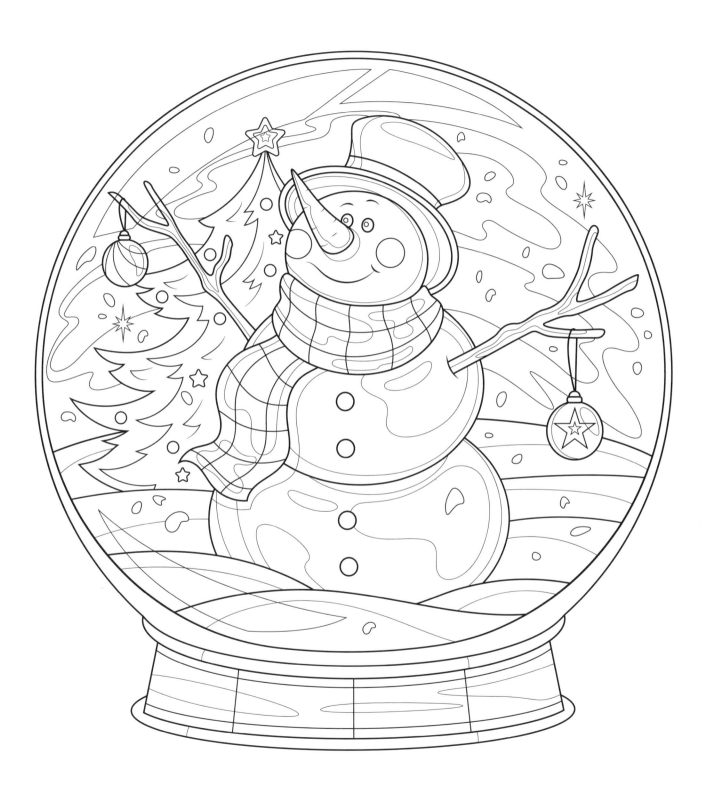

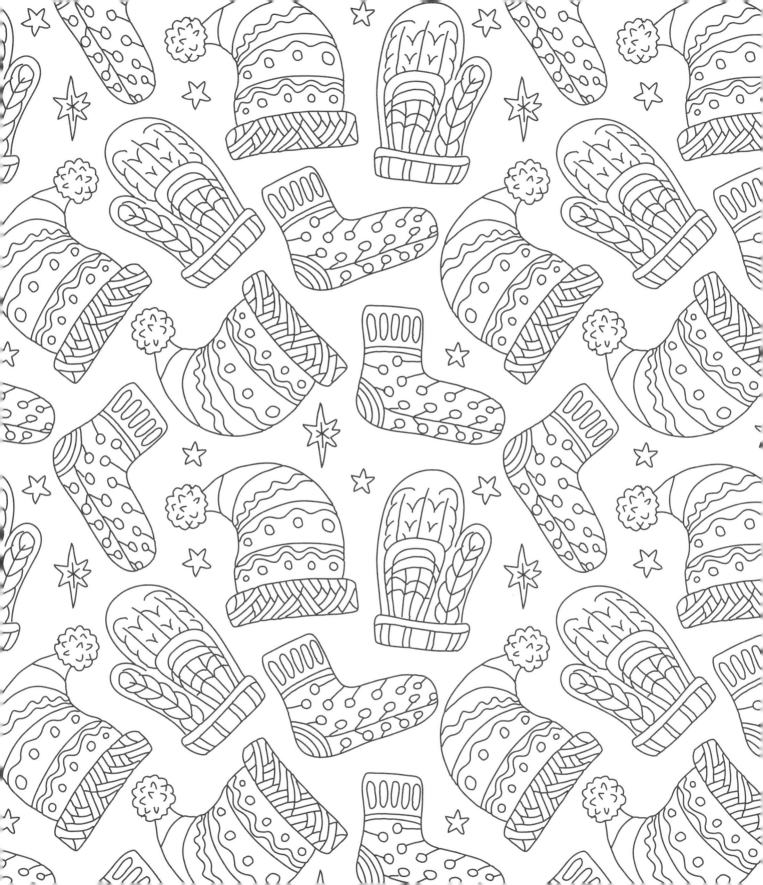

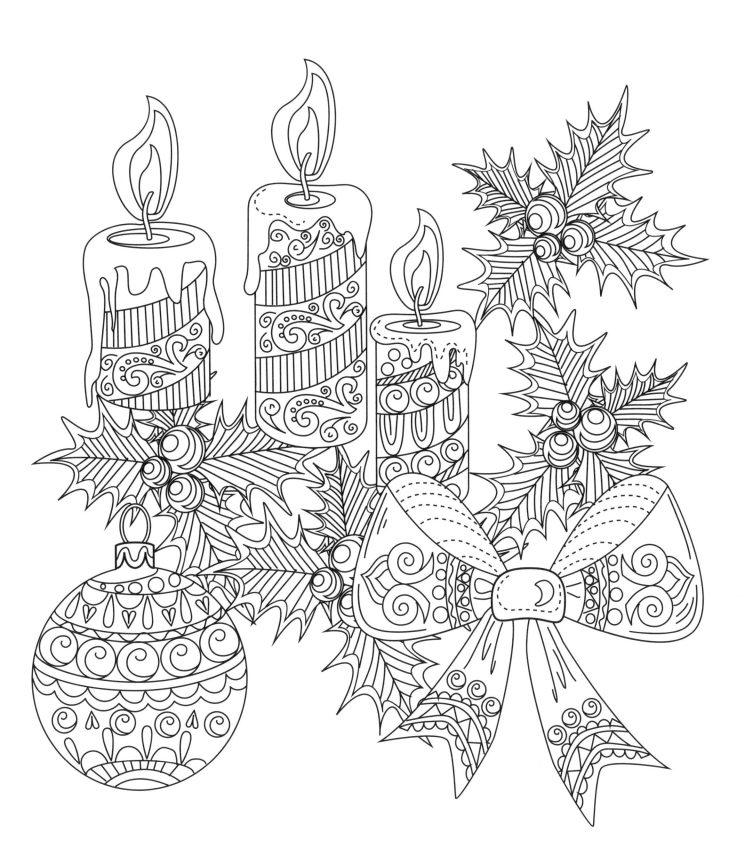

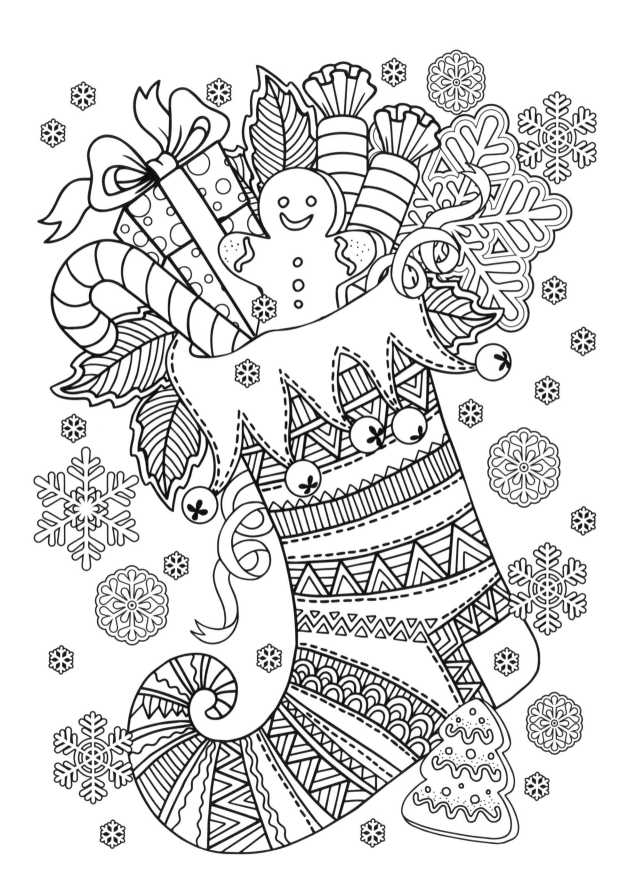

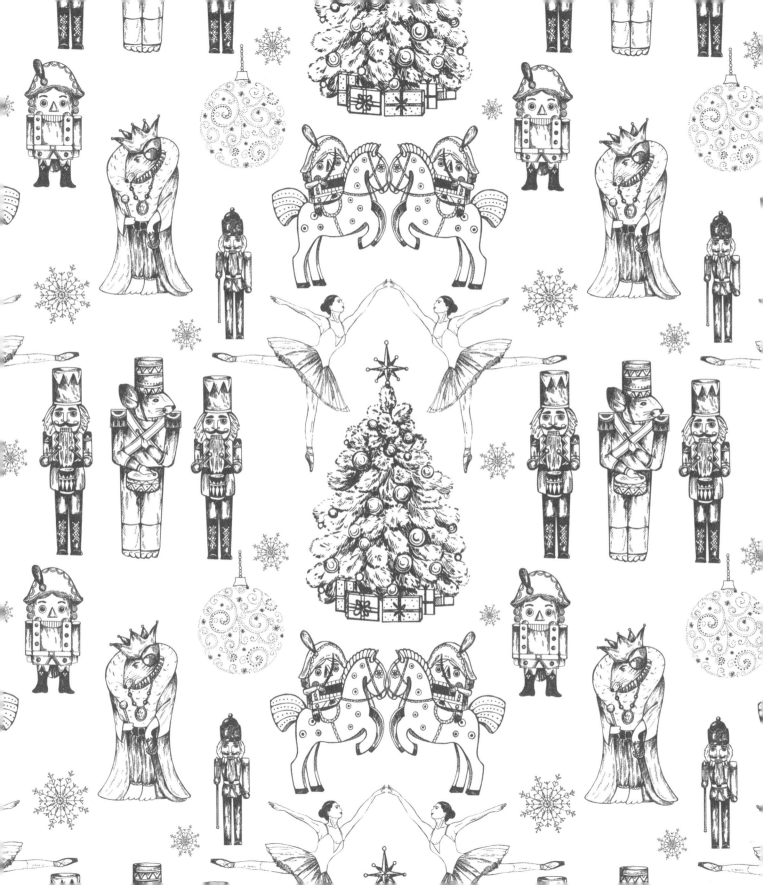

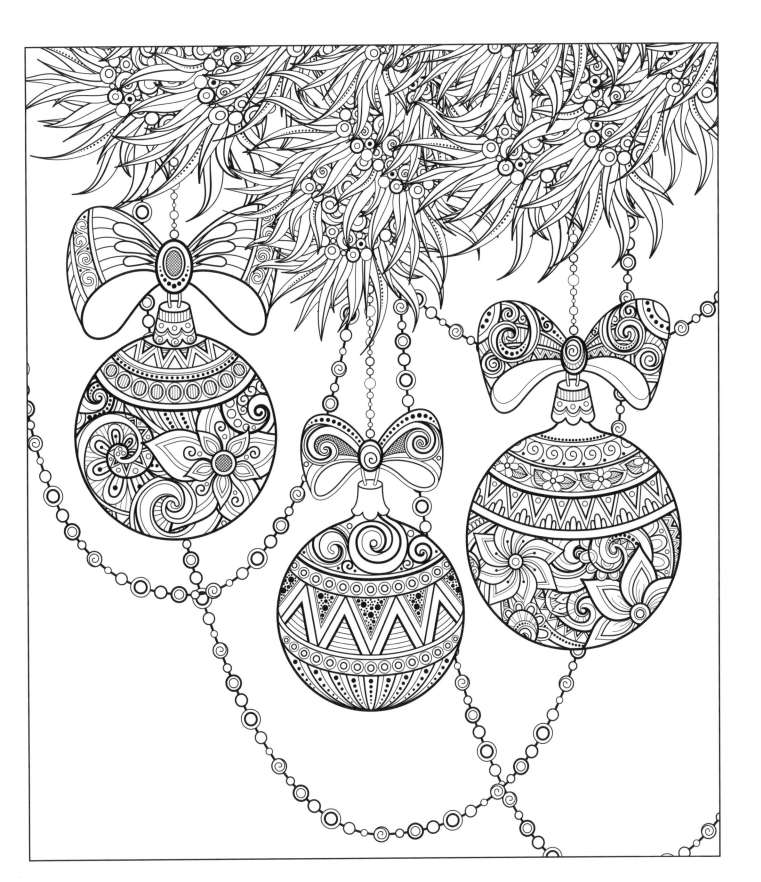

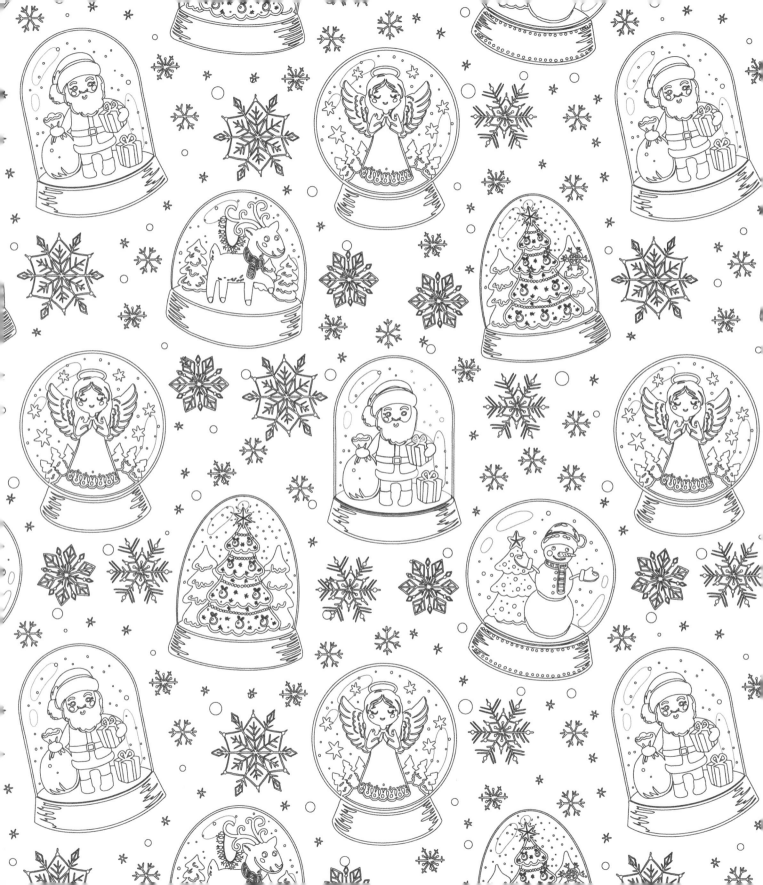

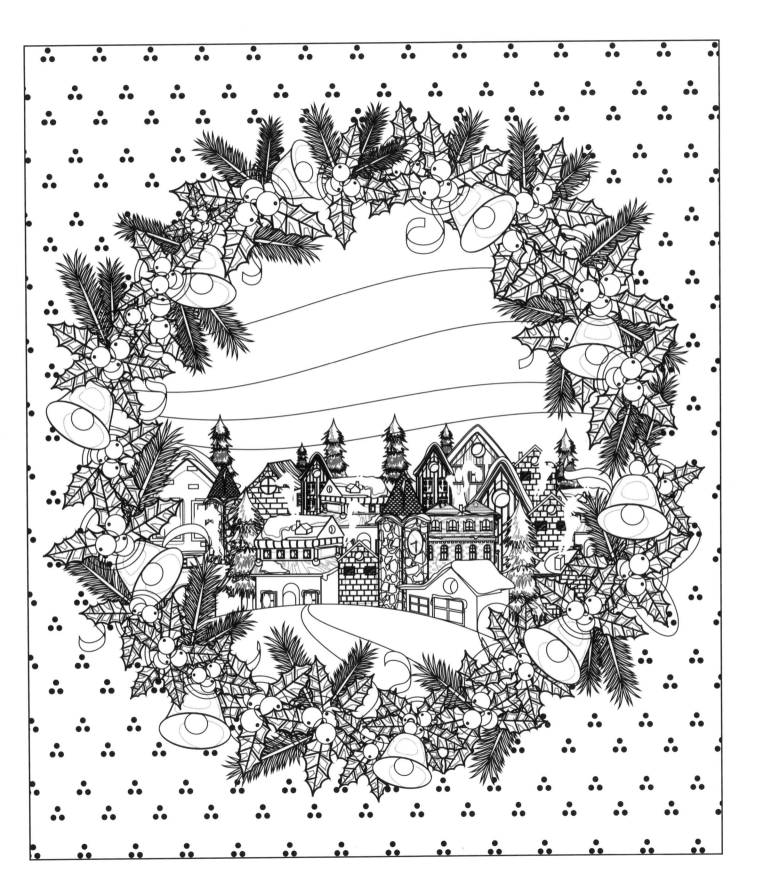

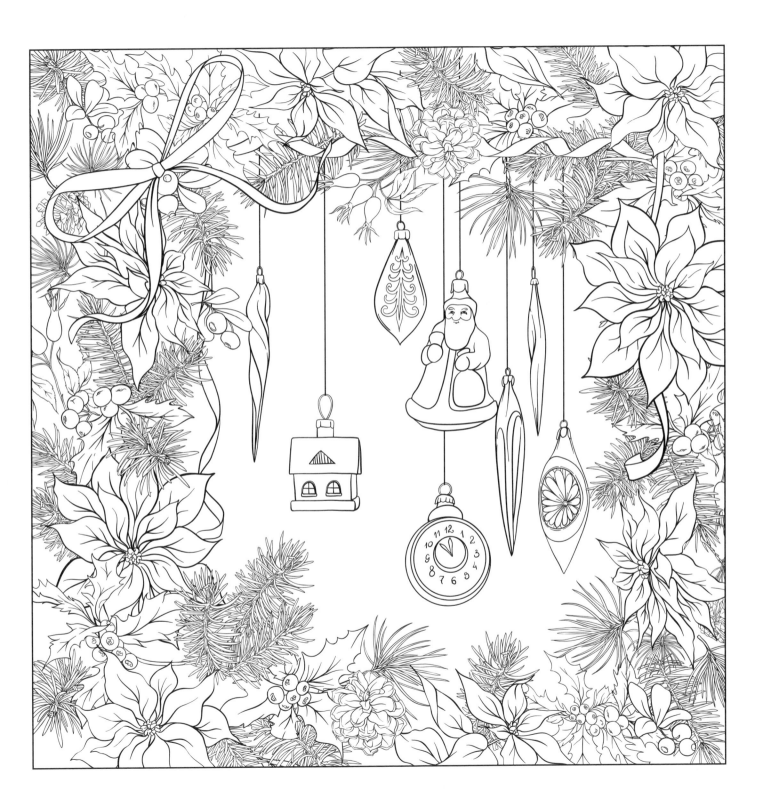

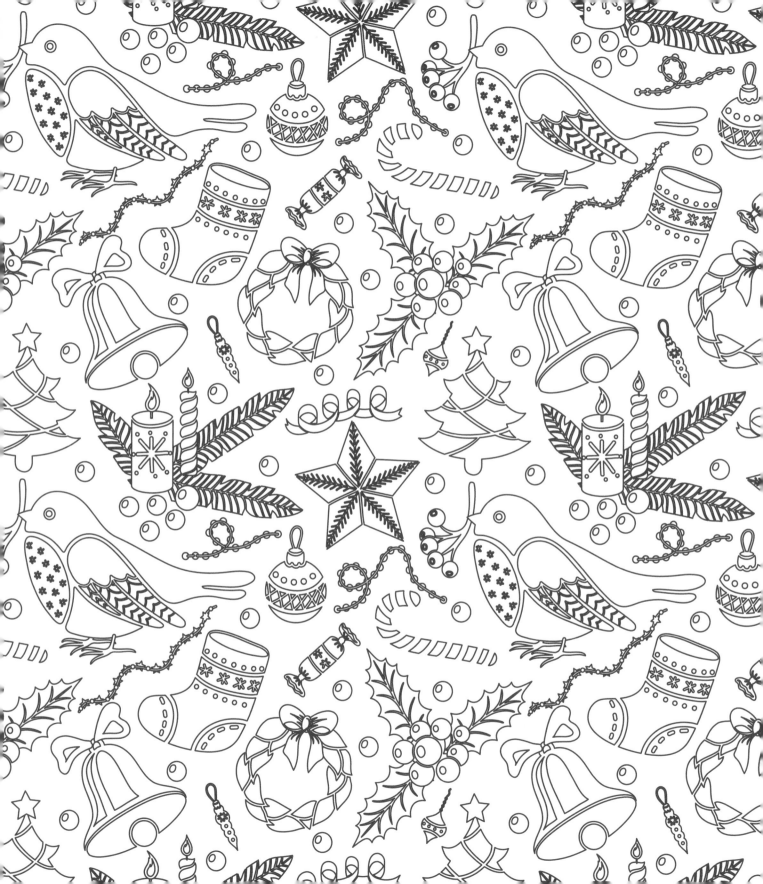

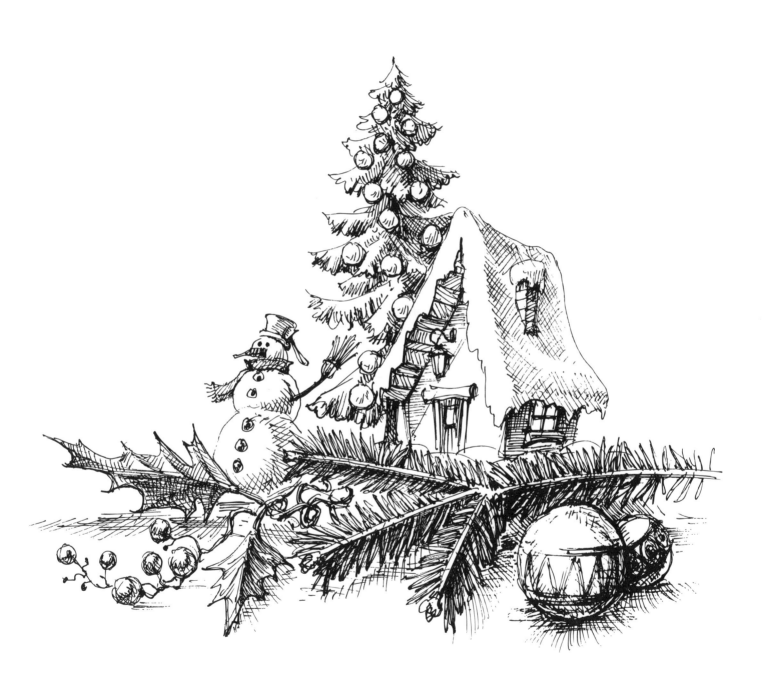

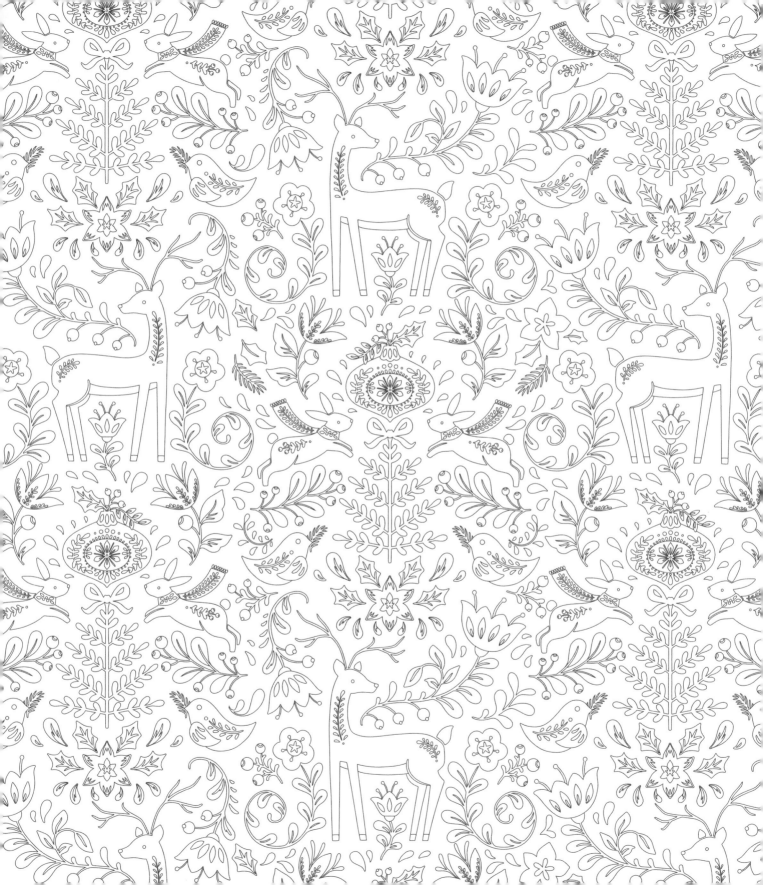

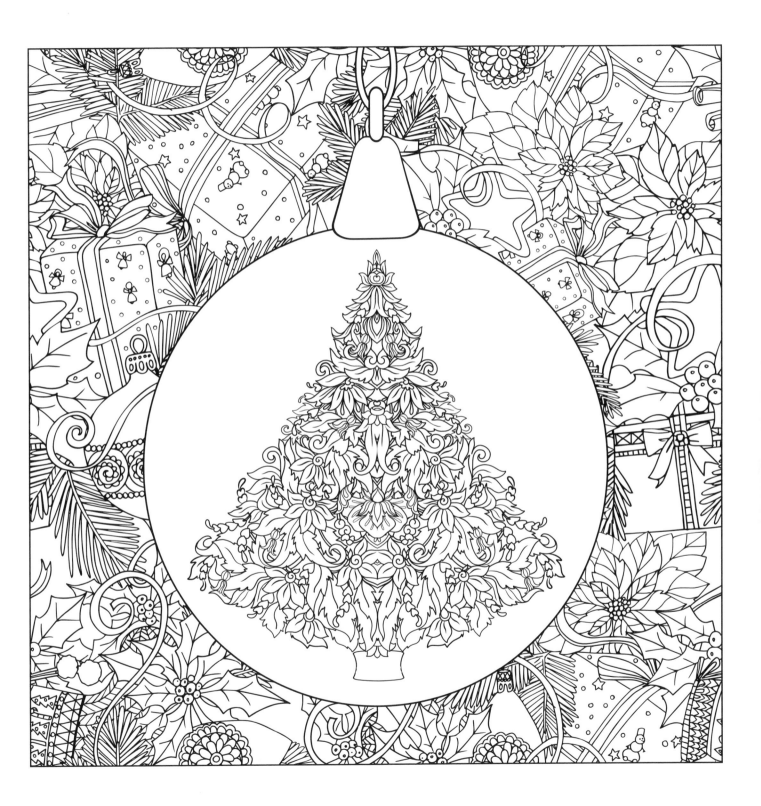

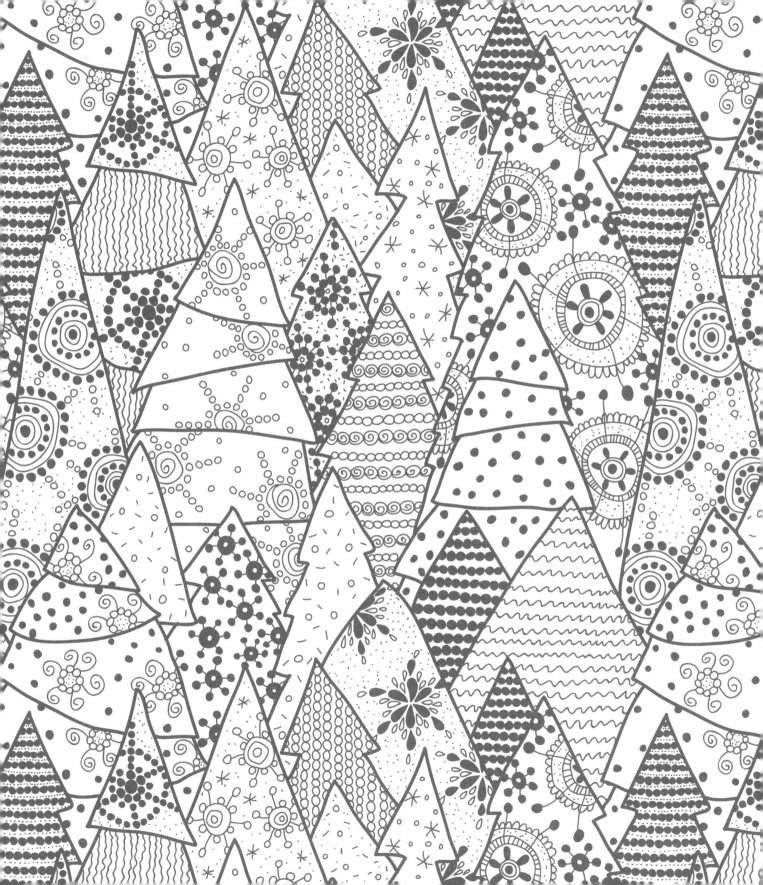

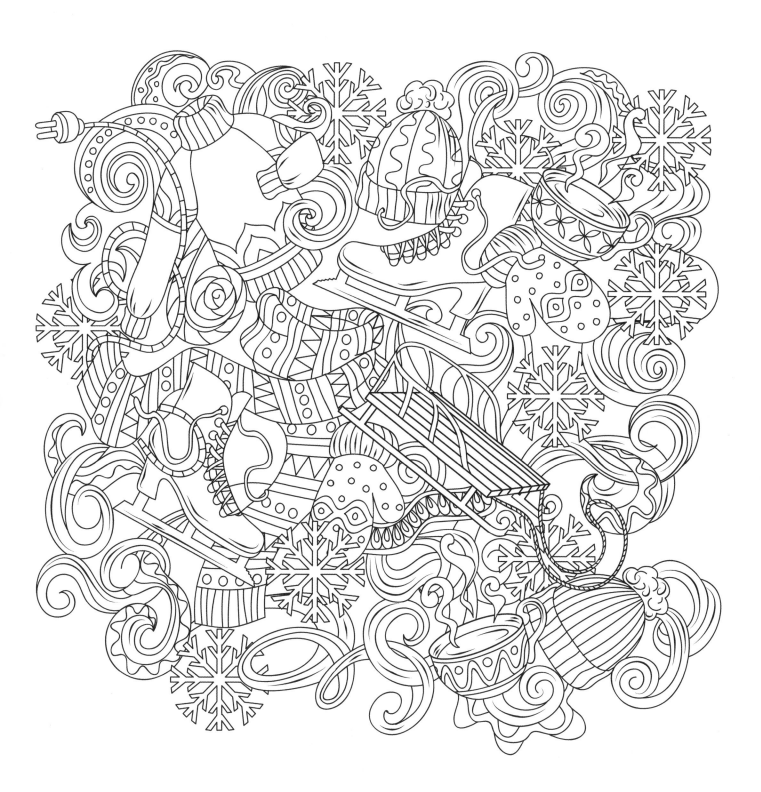

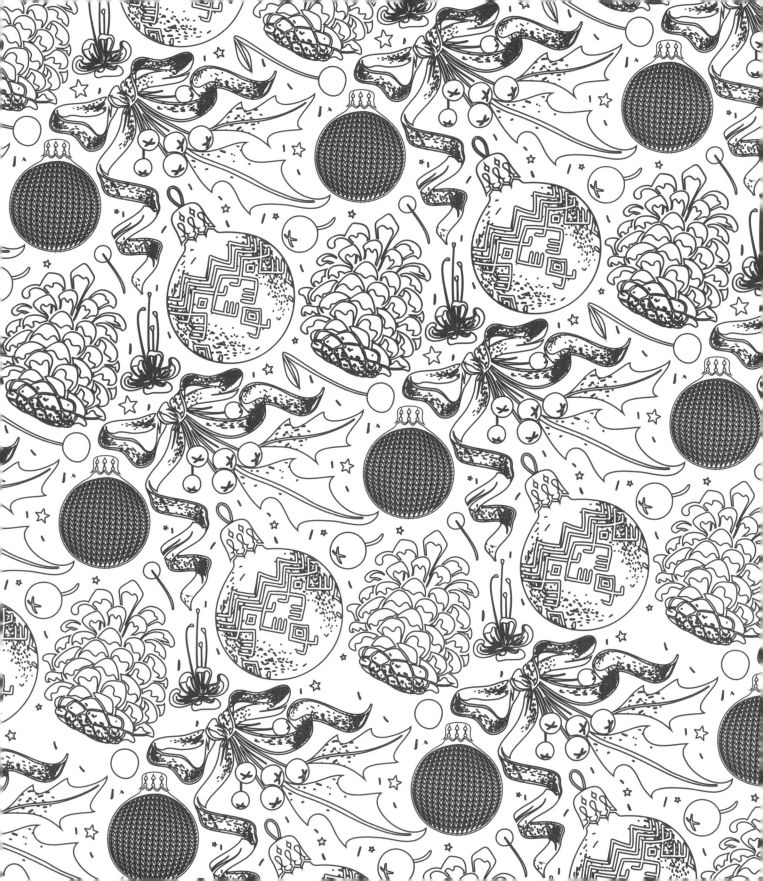

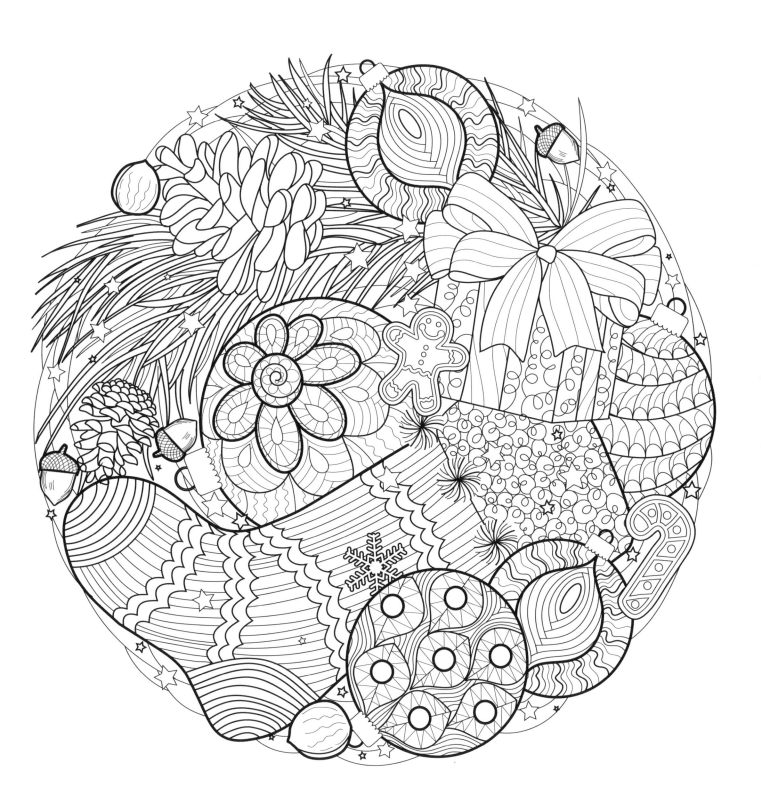

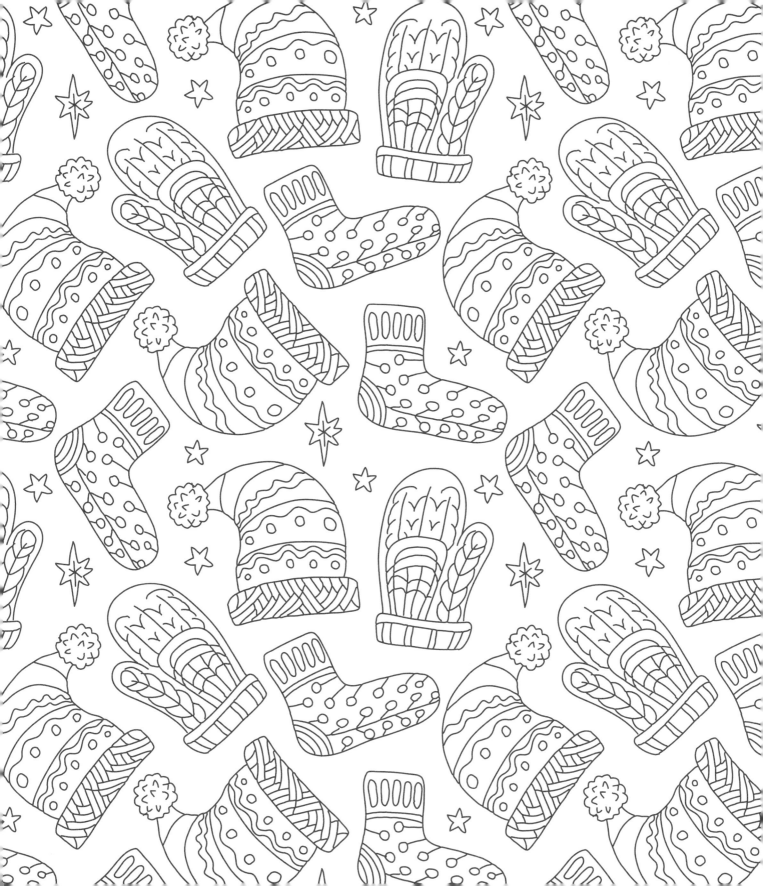

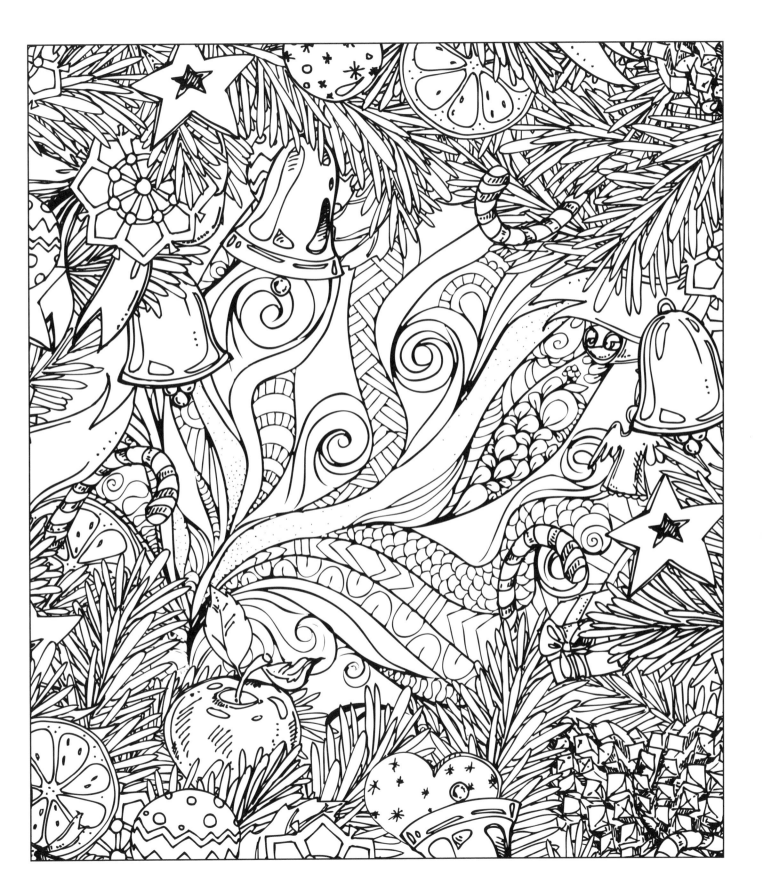

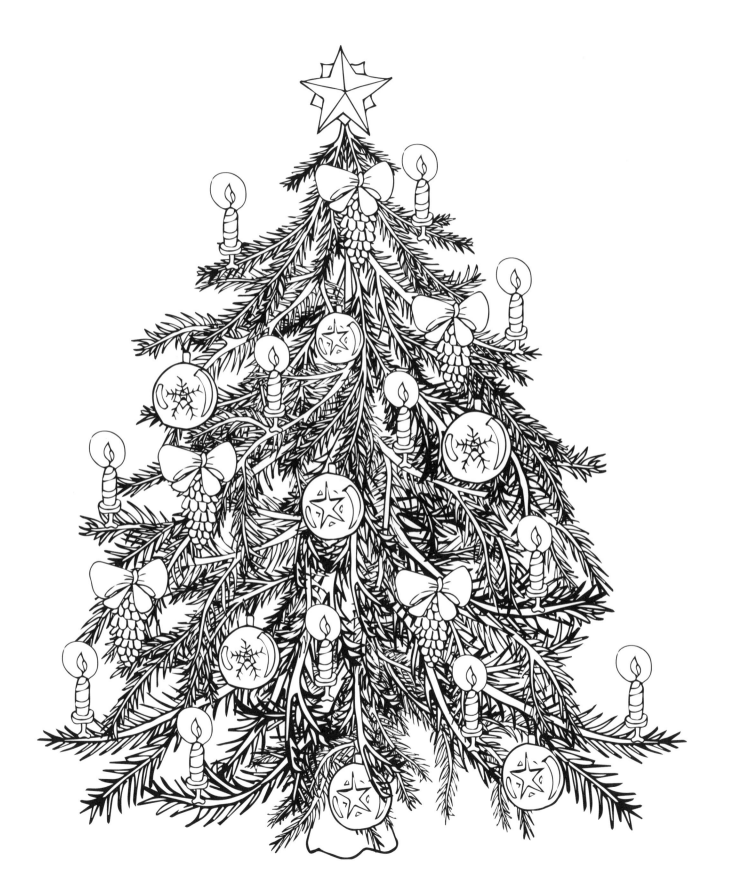

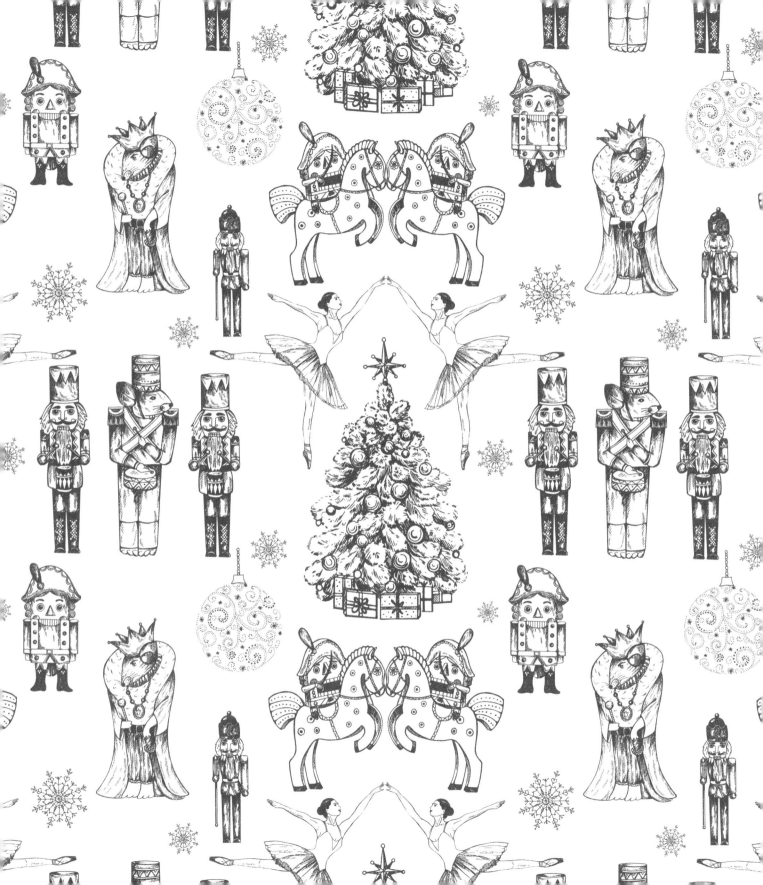

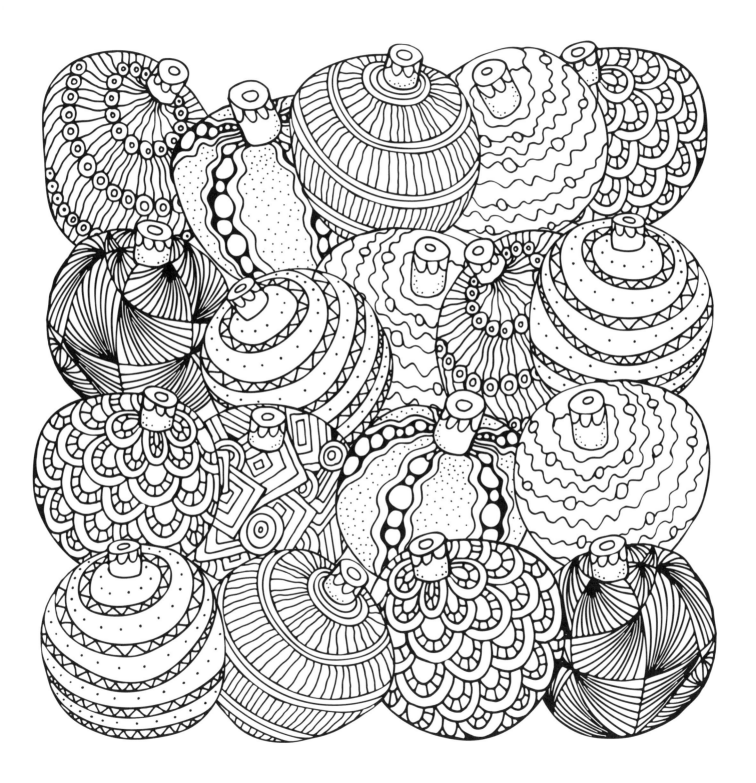

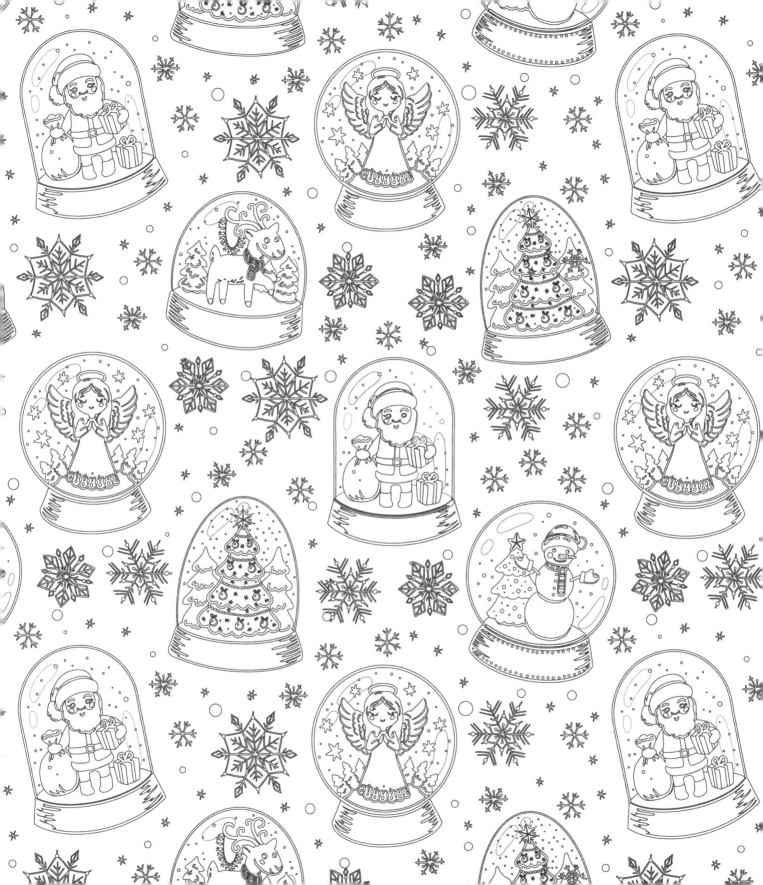

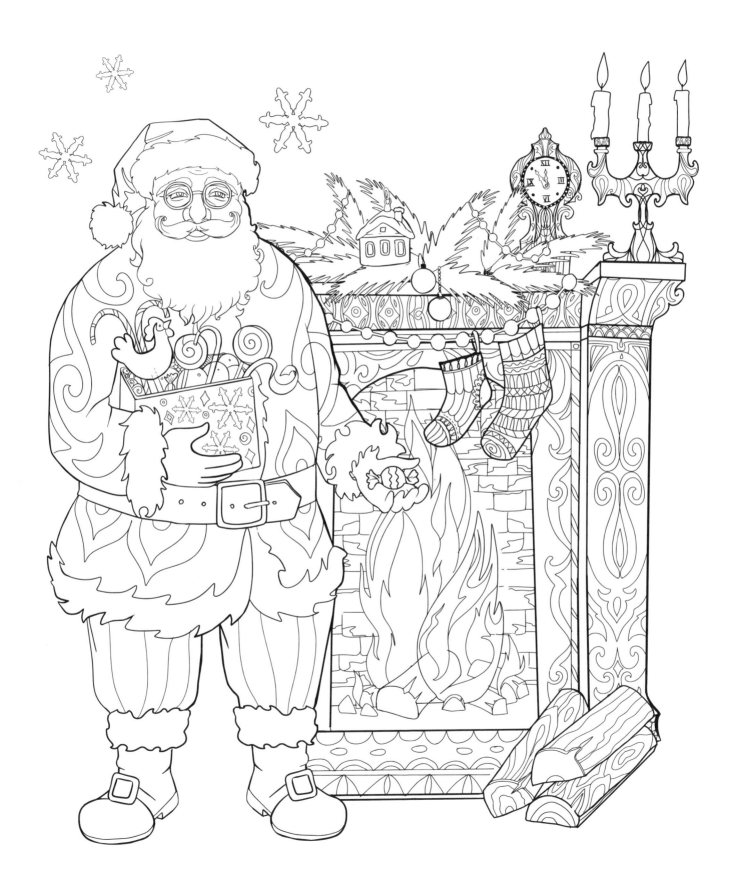

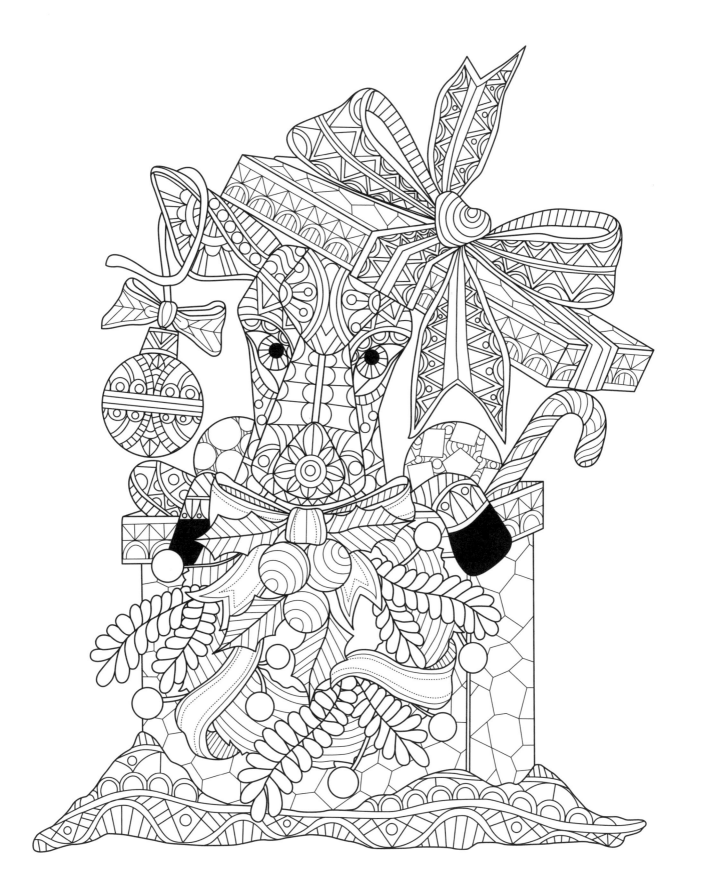

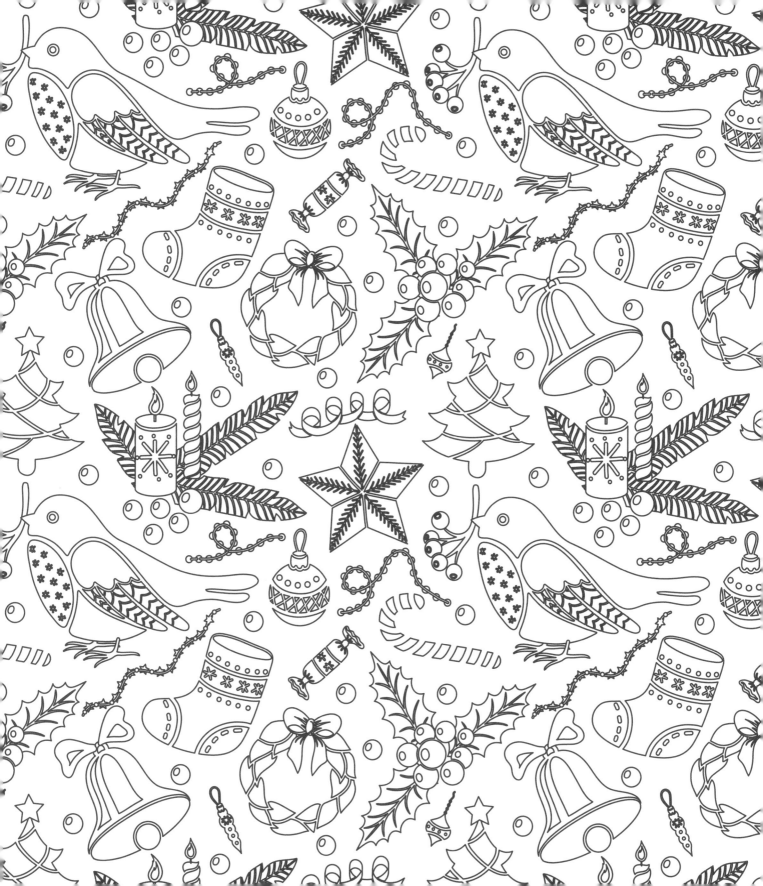

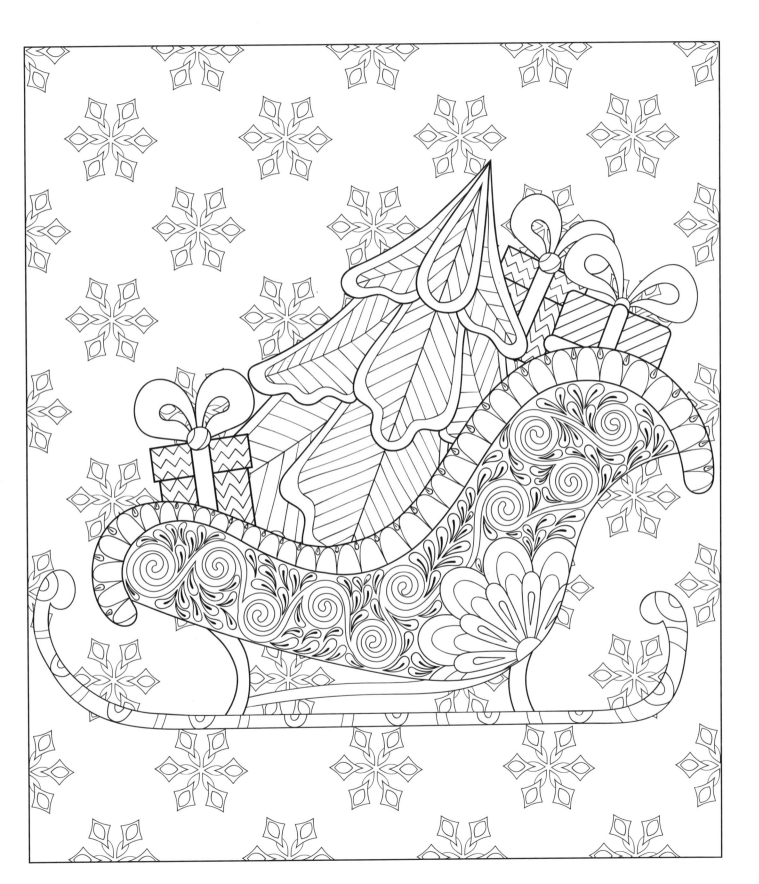

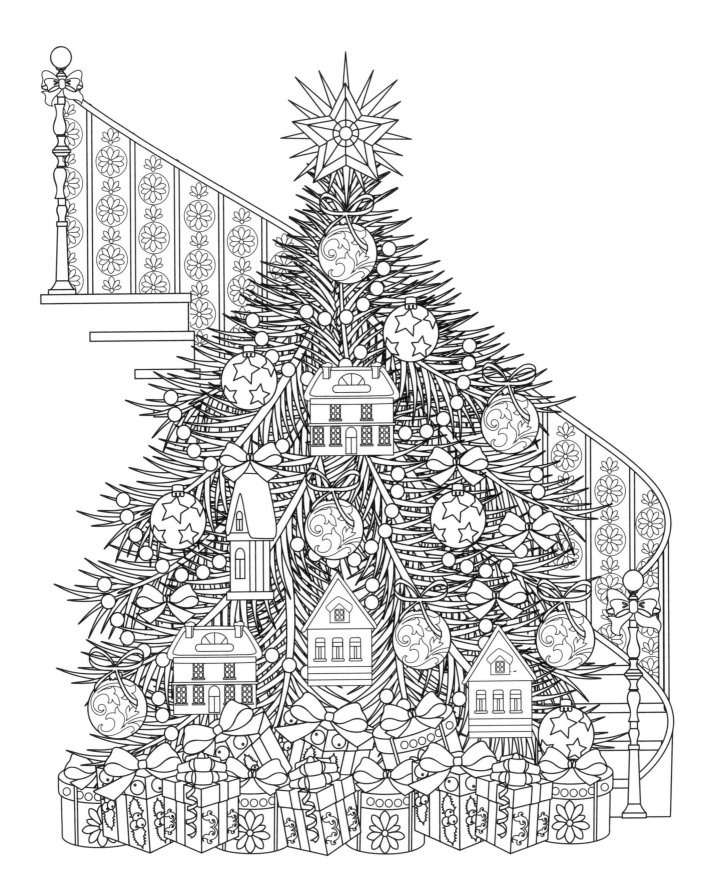

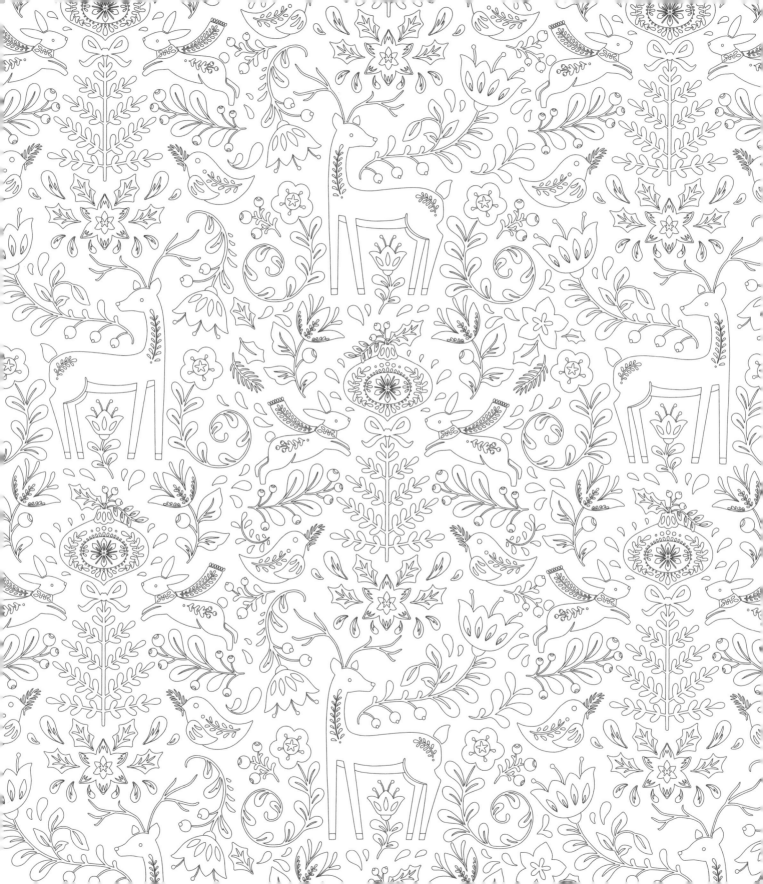

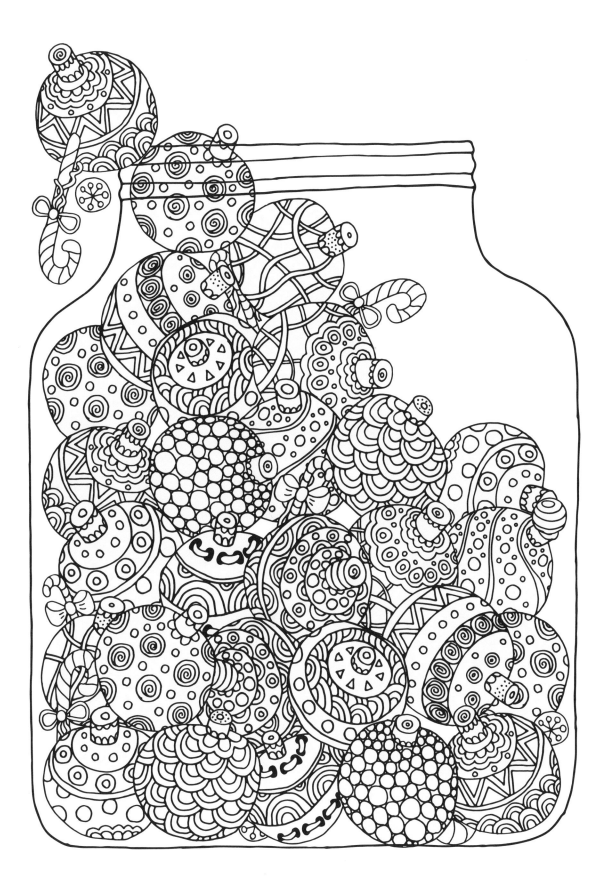

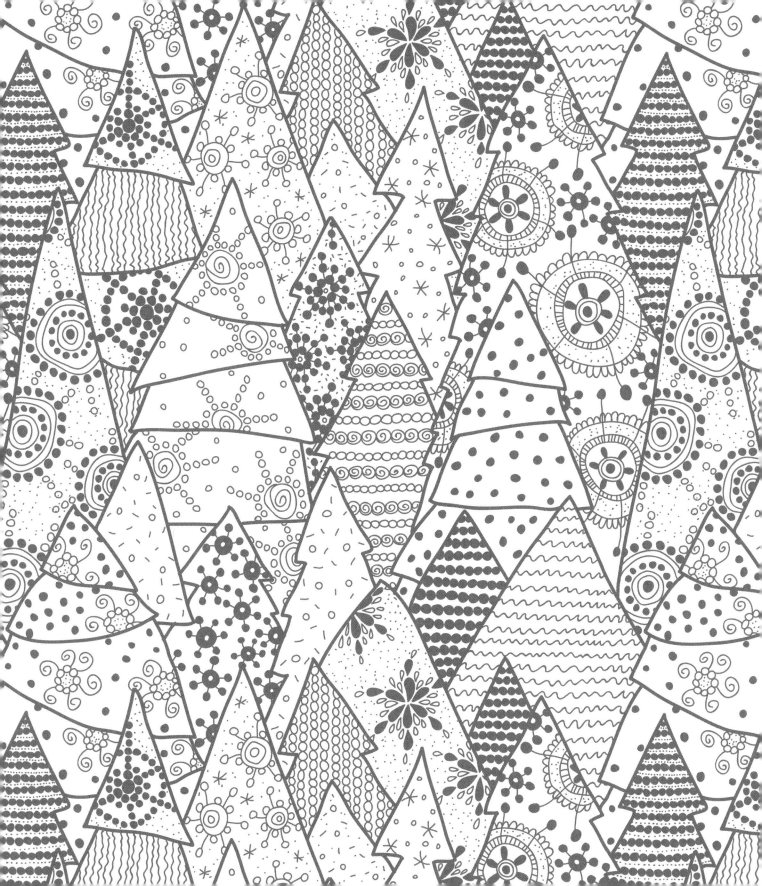

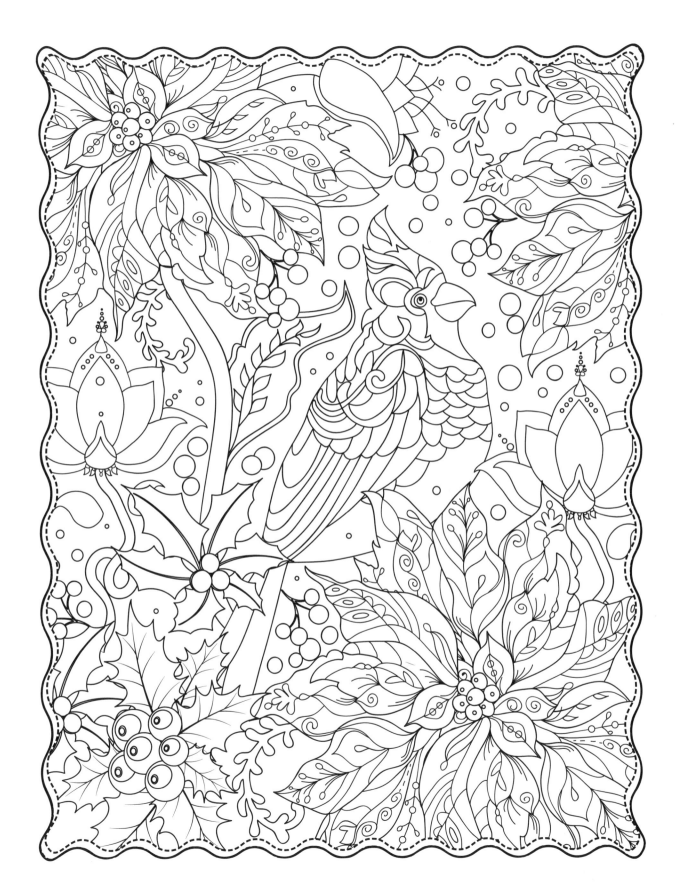

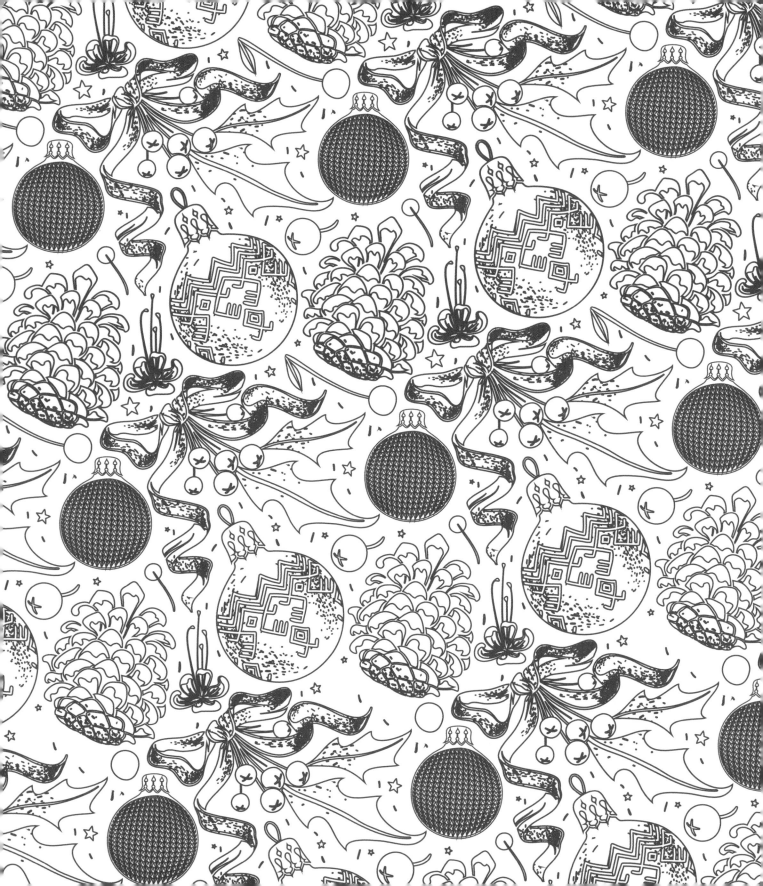

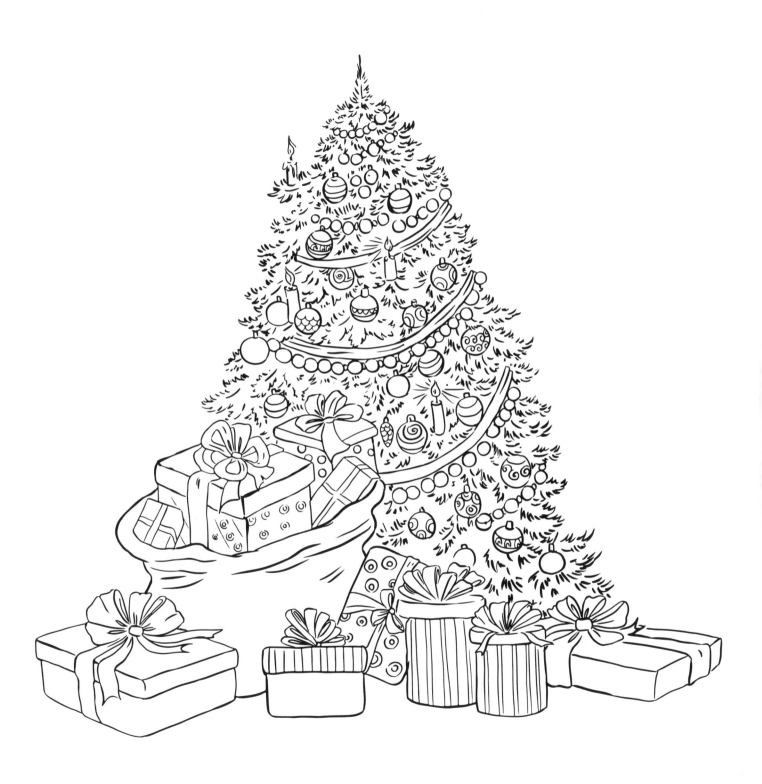

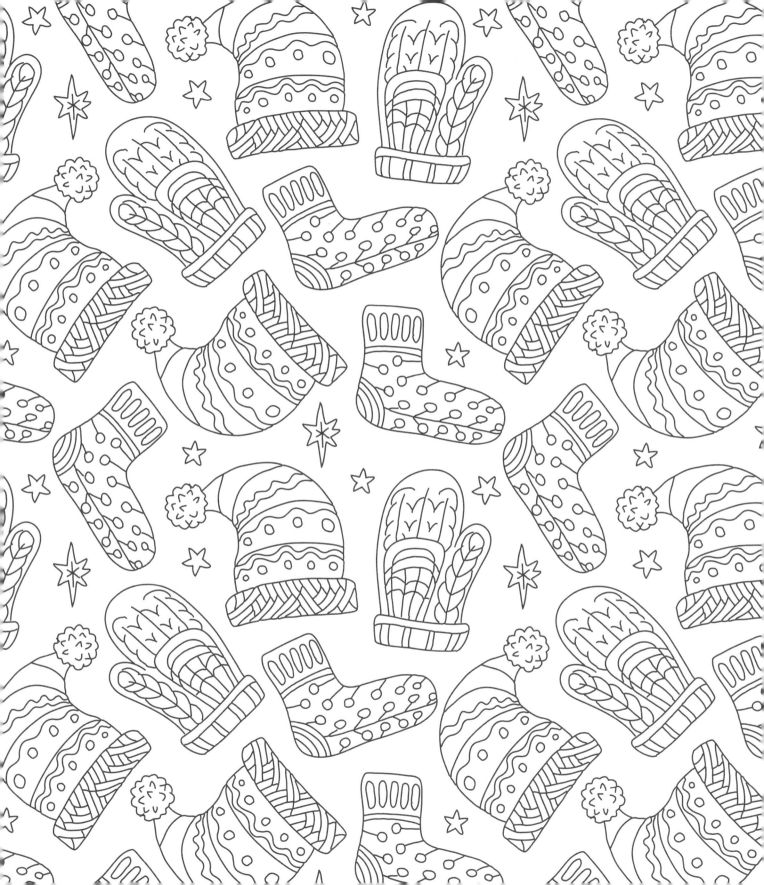

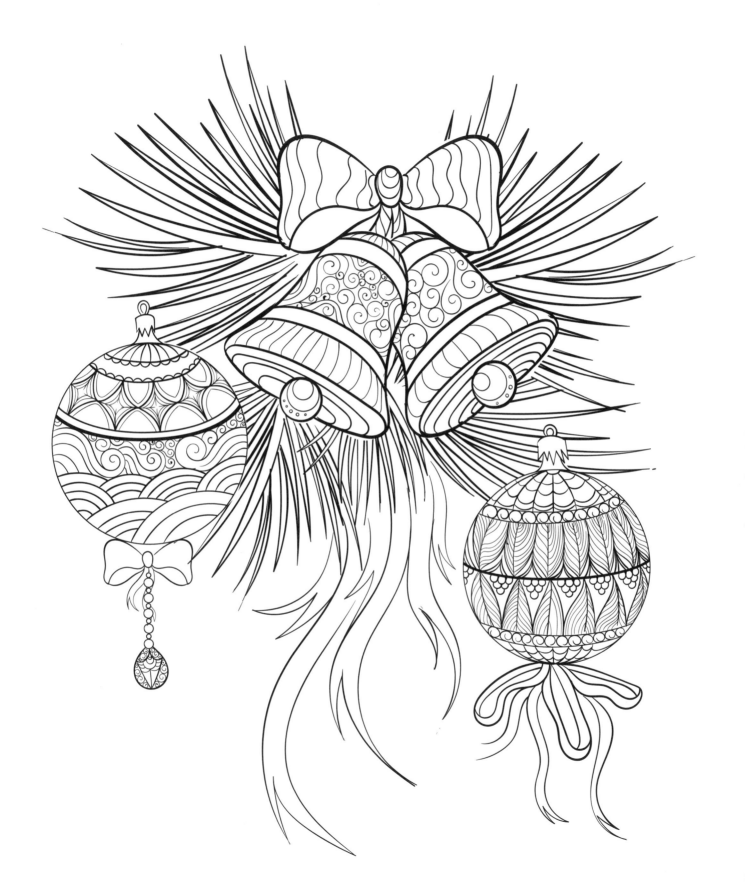

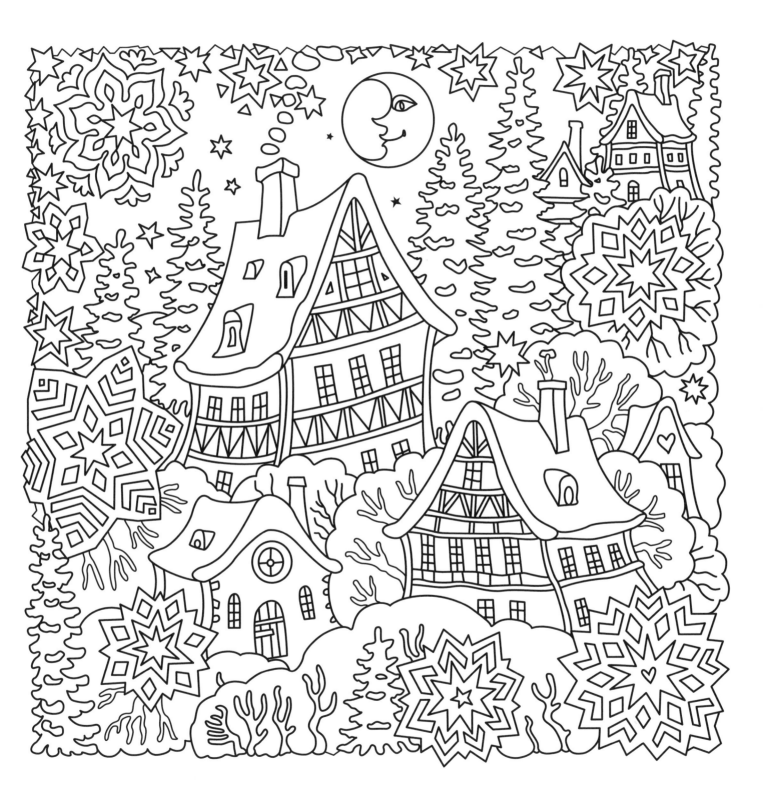

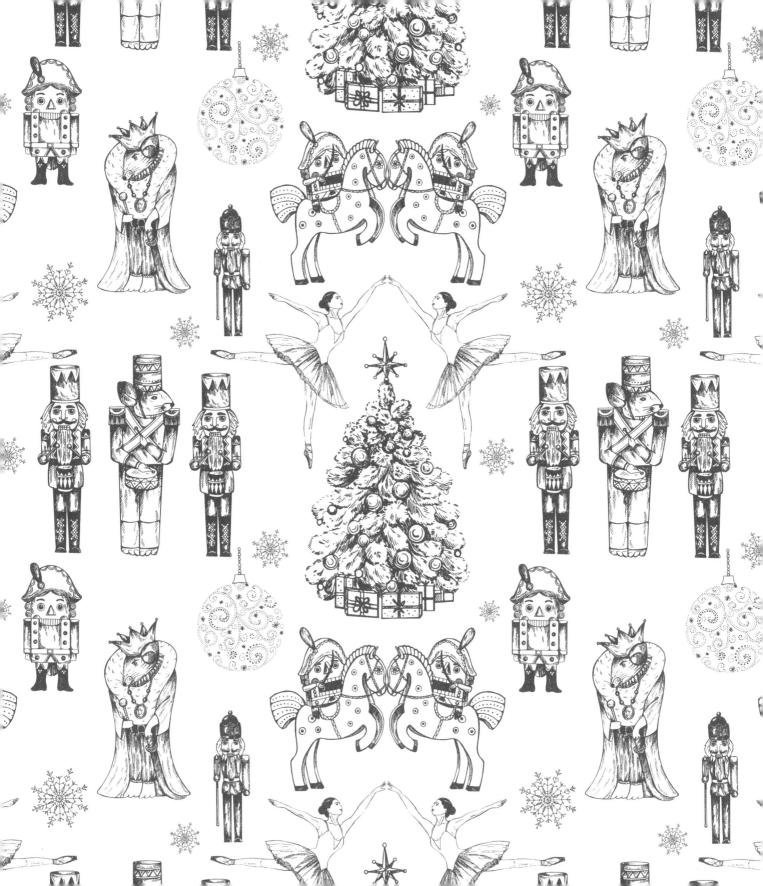

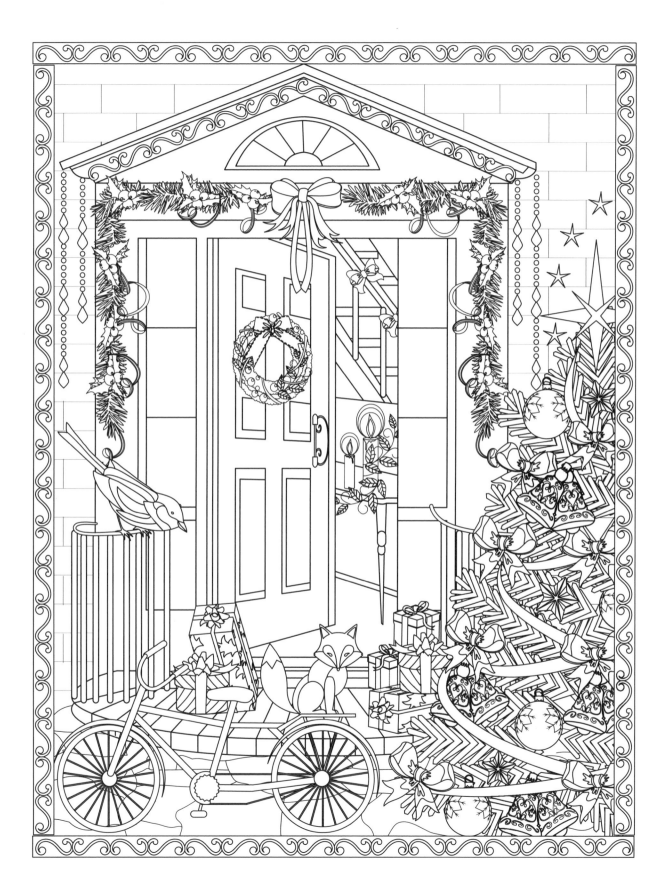

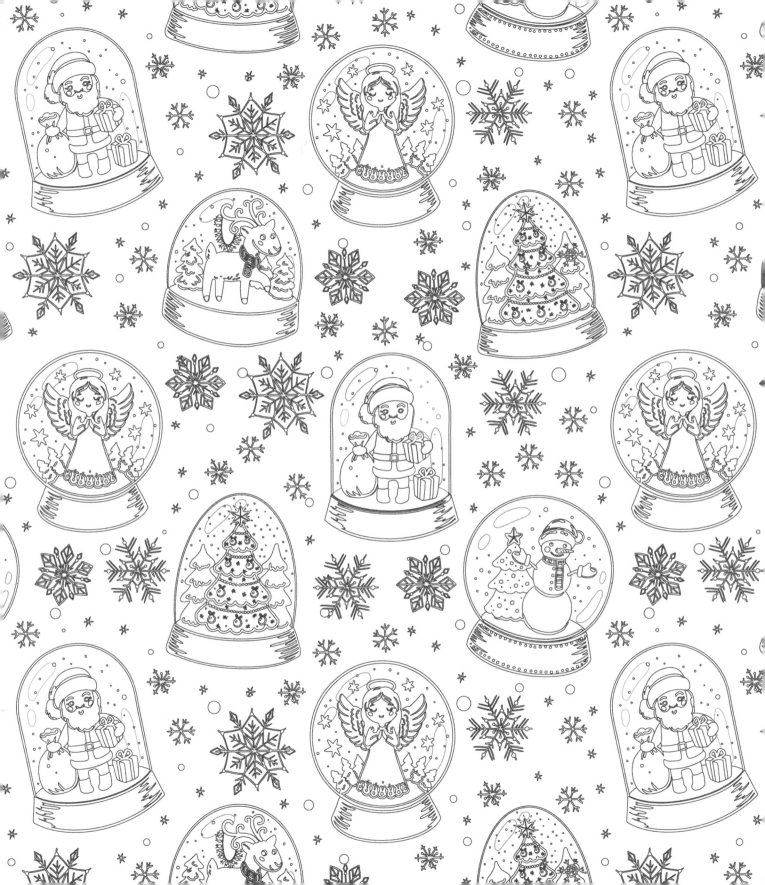

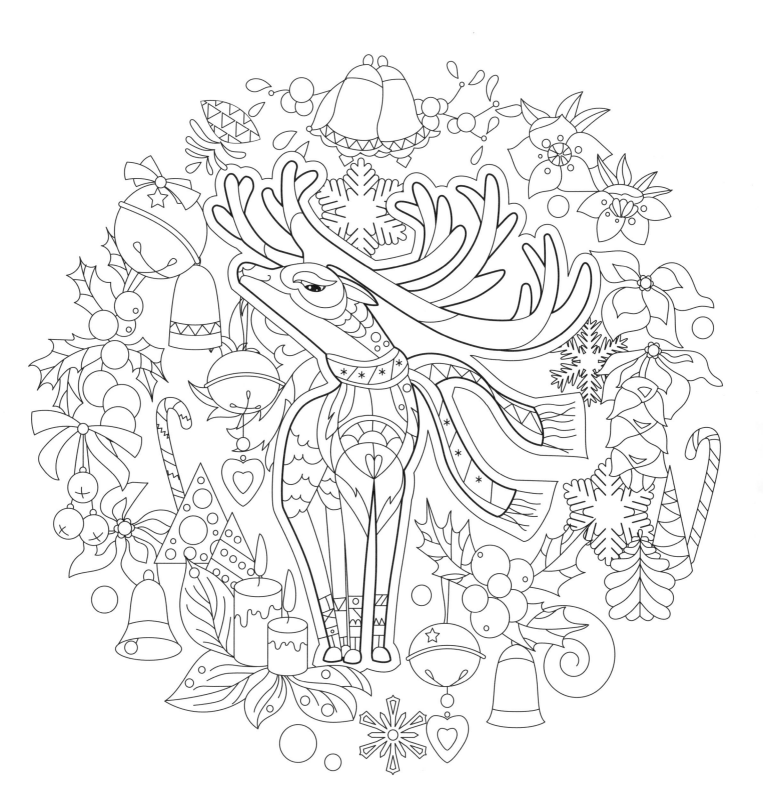

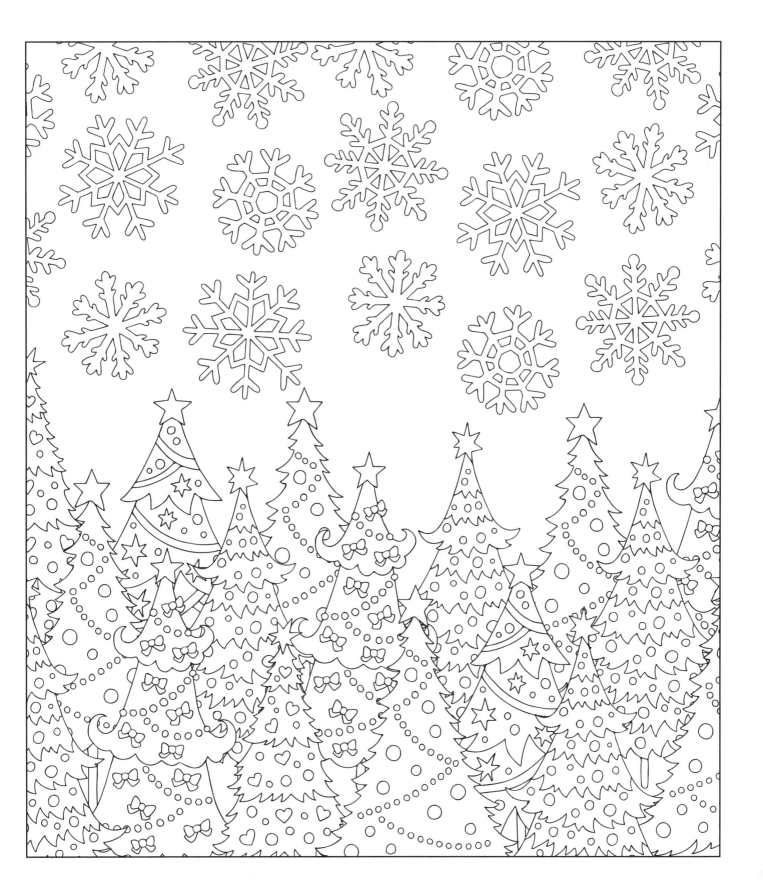

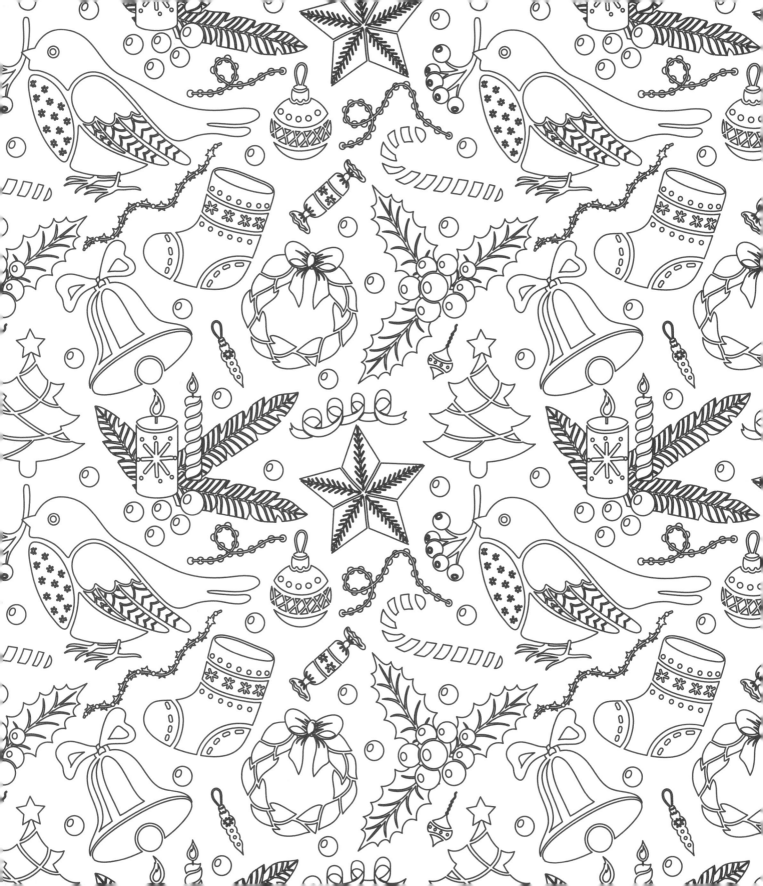

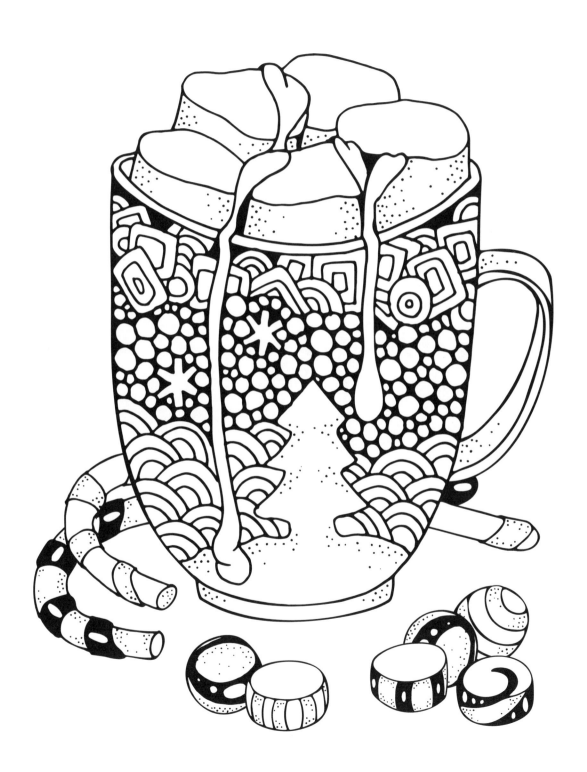

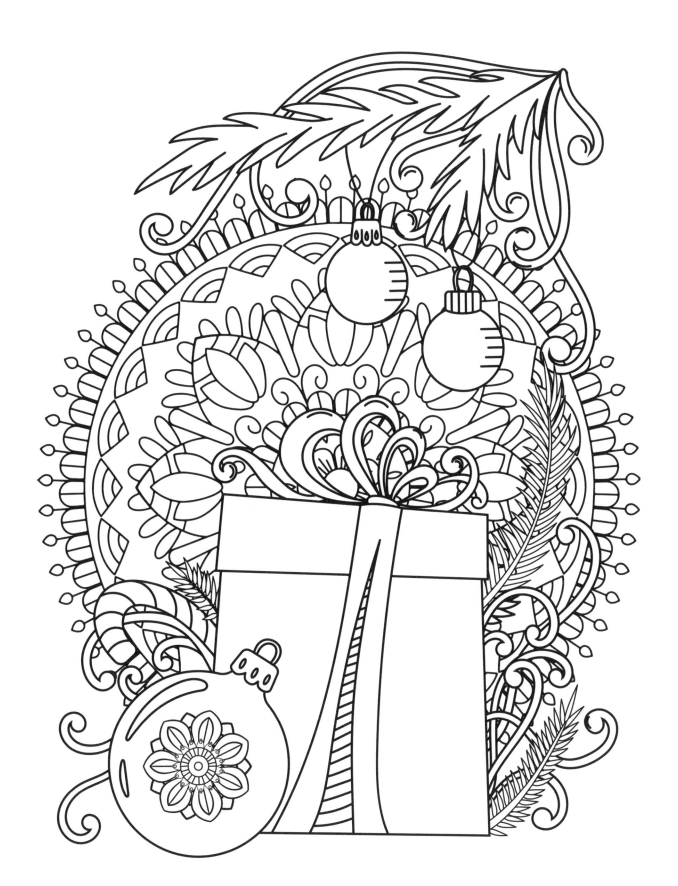

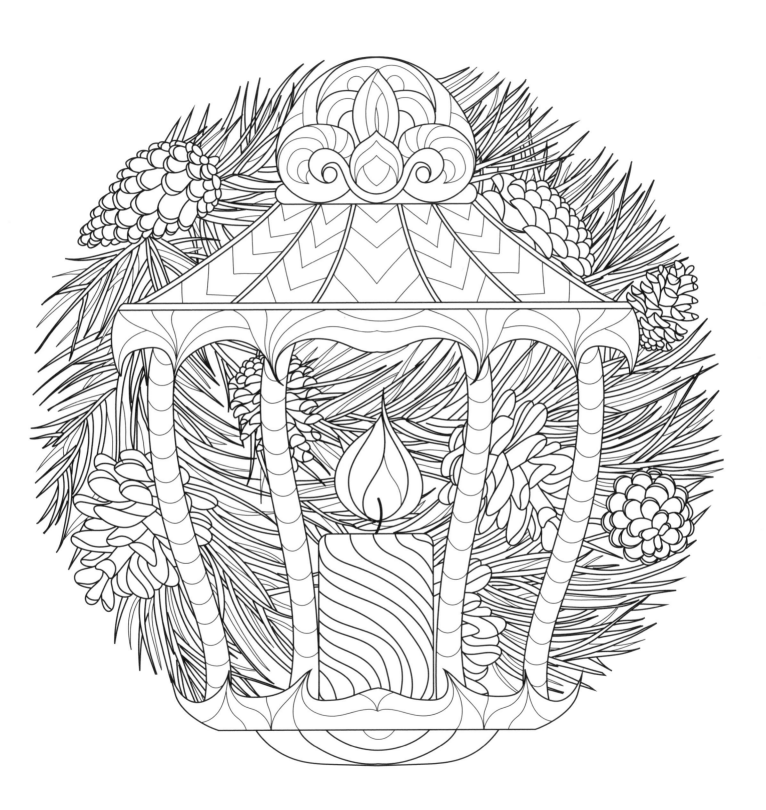

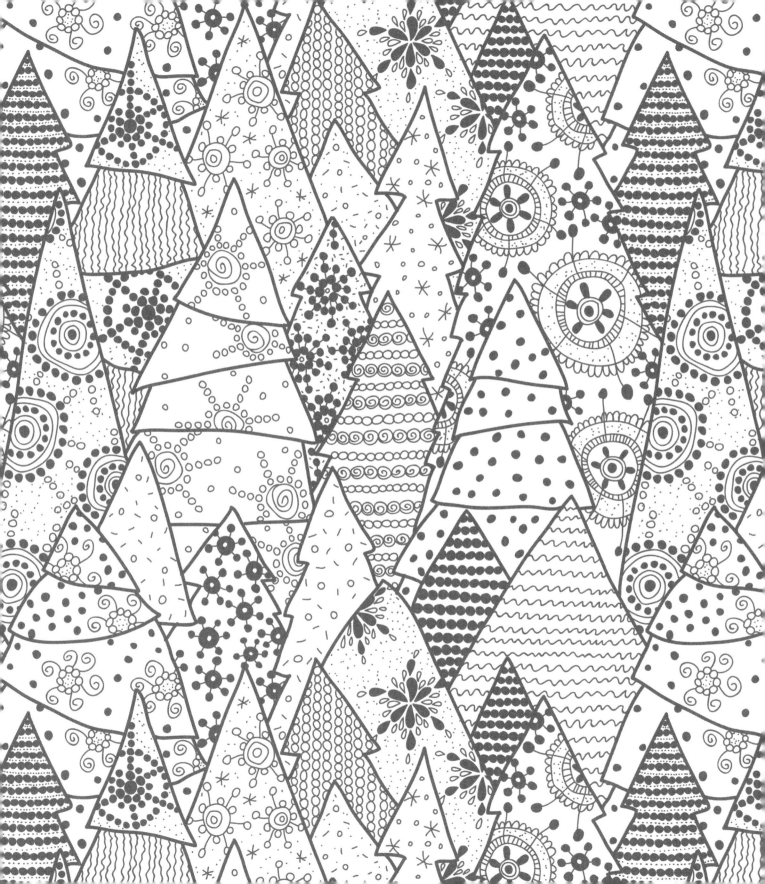

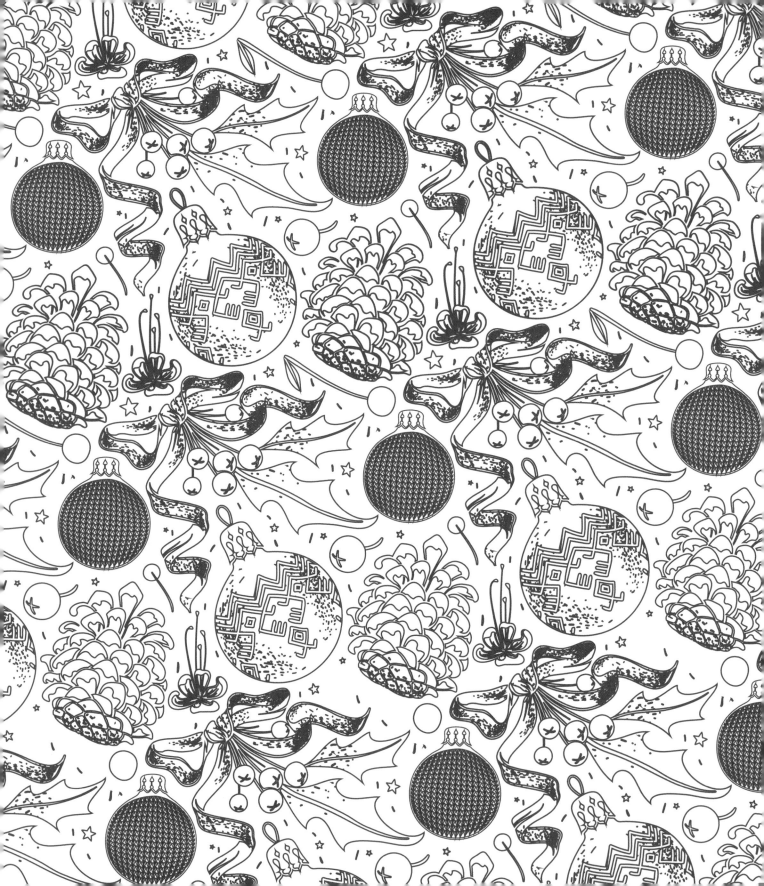

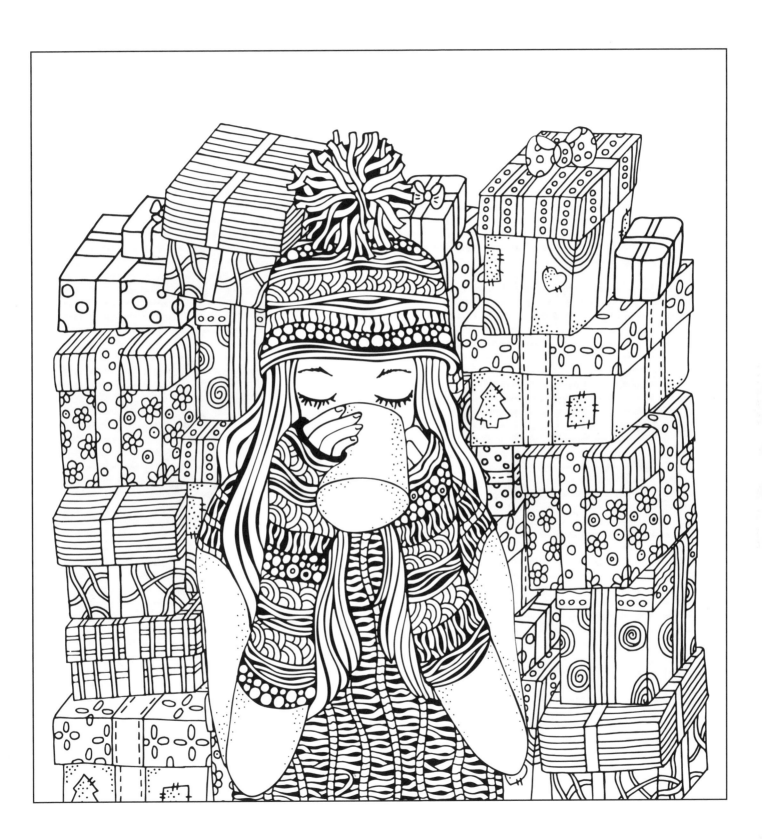

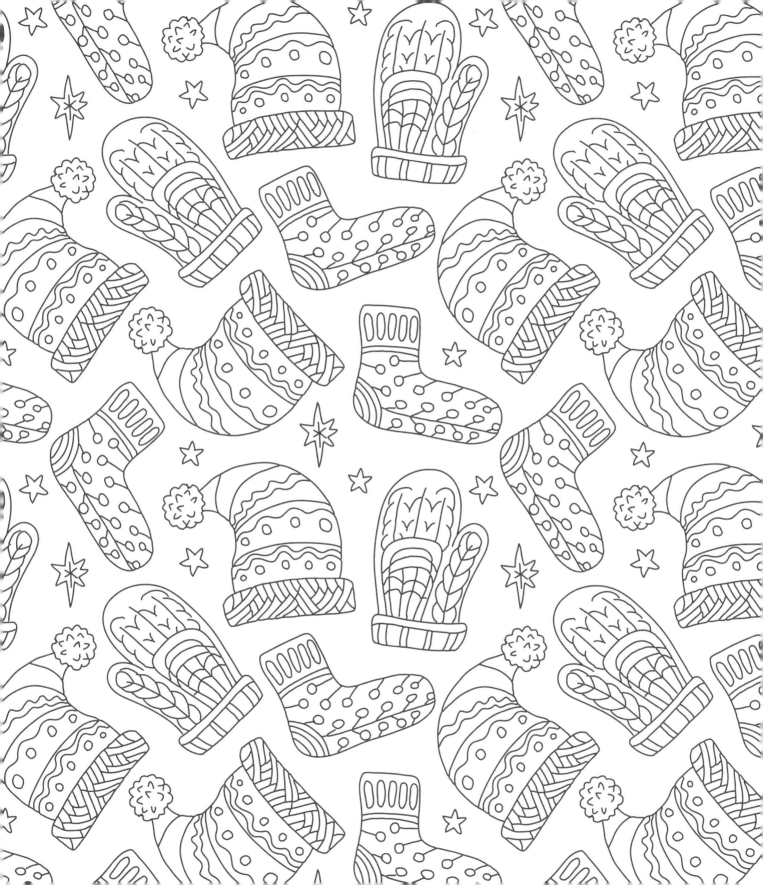

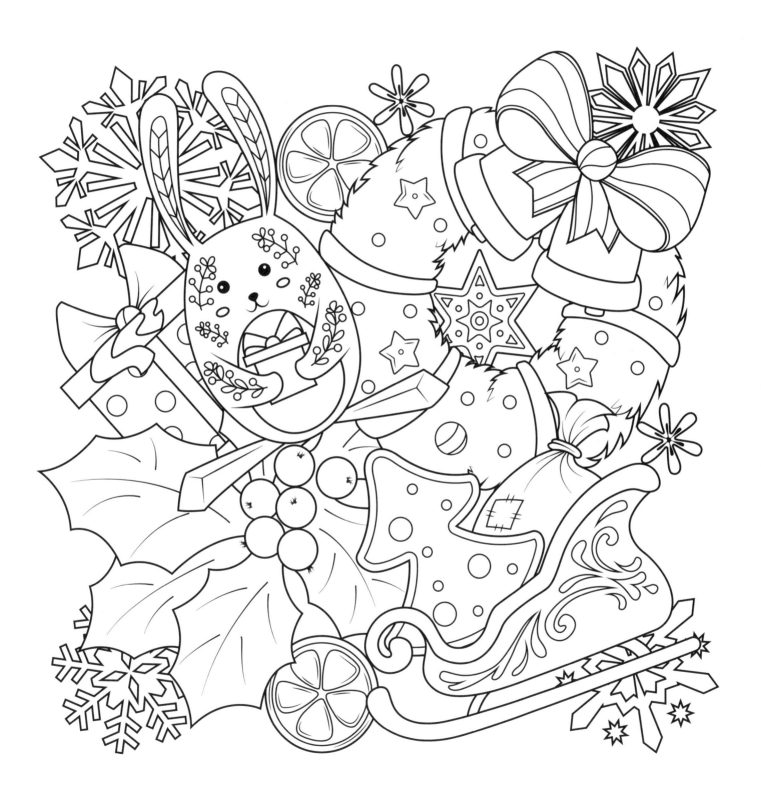

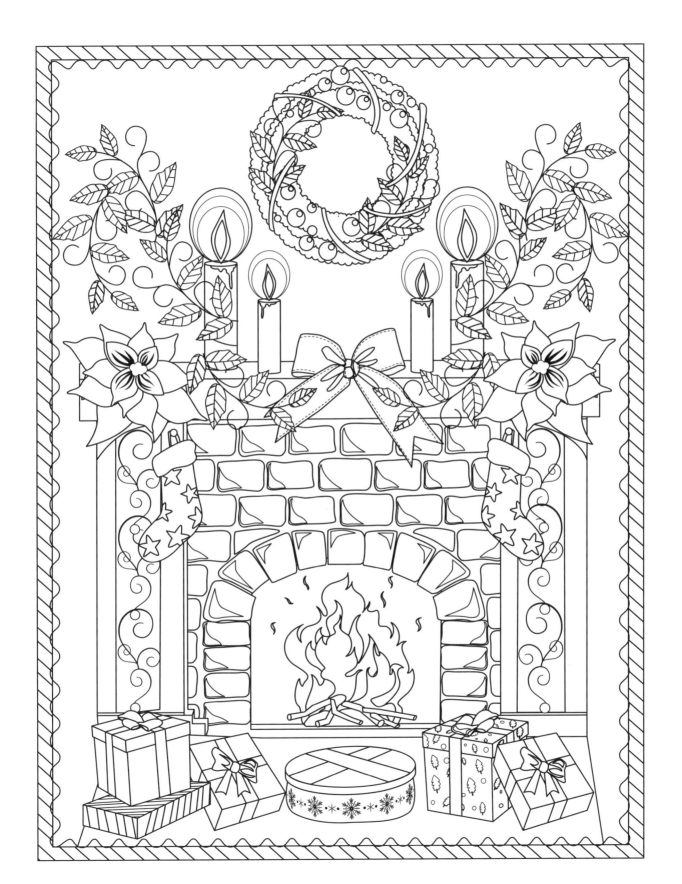

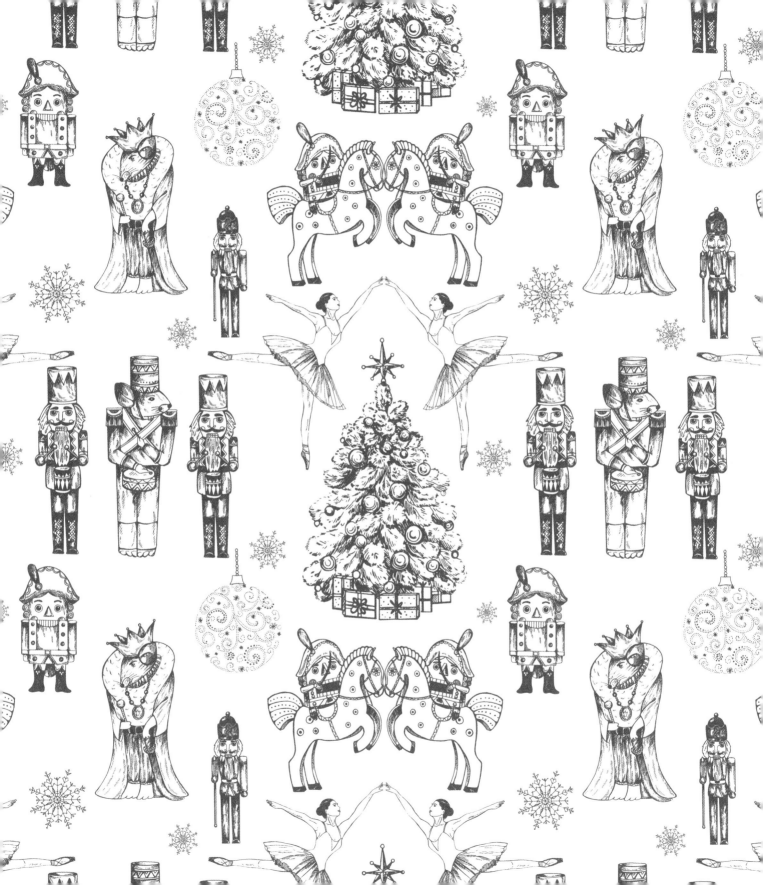

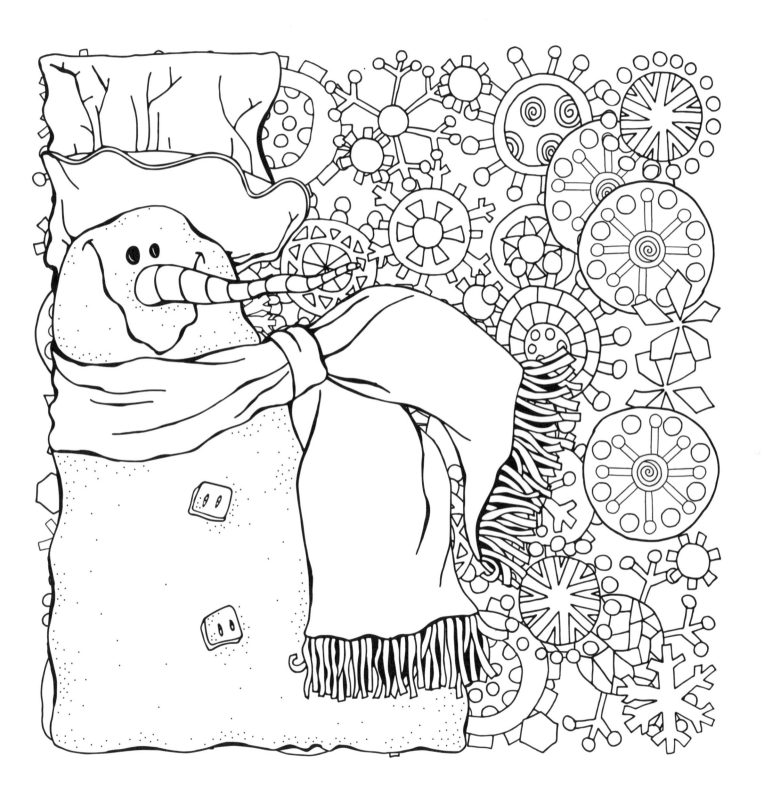

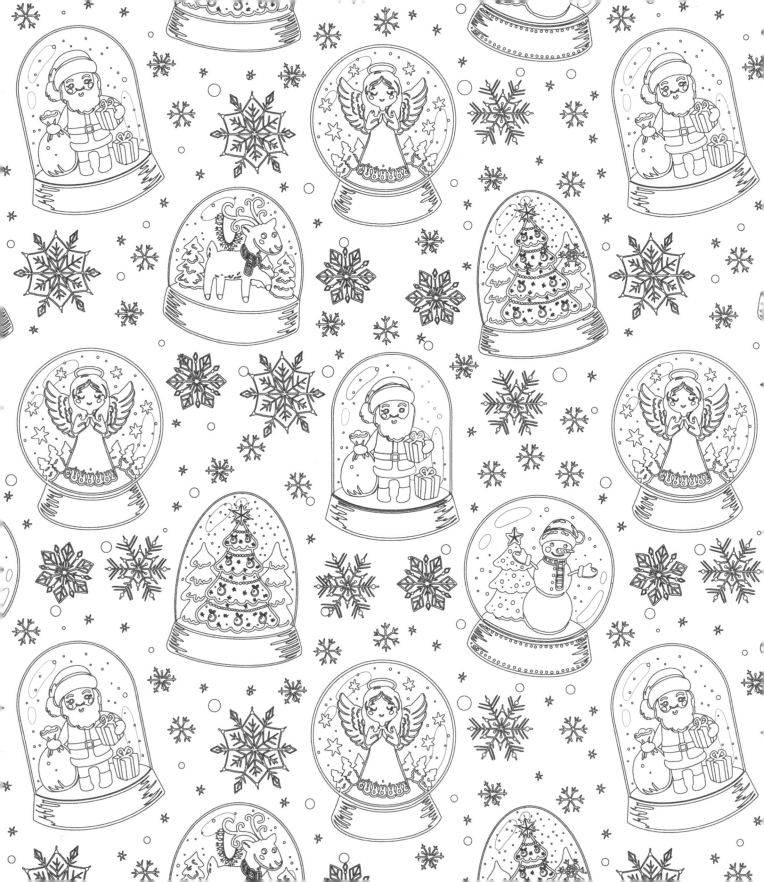

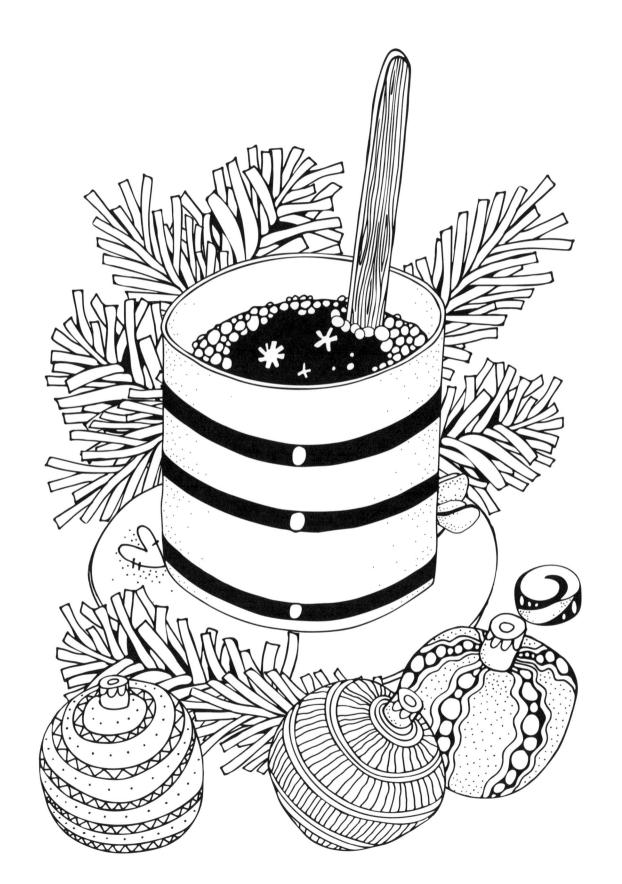

Quarto

© 2023 Quarto Publishing Group USA Inc.

This edition published in 2023 by Chartwell Books,
an imprint of The Quarto Group
142 West 36th Street, 4th Floor
New York, NY 10018 USA
 T (212) 779-4972 F (212) 779-6058
www.Quarto.com

10 9 8 7 6 5 4 3 2 1

Chartwell titles are also available at discount for retail, wholesale, promotional, and bulk purchase. For details, contact the Special Sales Manager by email at specialsales@quarto.com or by mail at The Quarto Group, Attn: Special Sales Manager, 100 Cummings Center Suite 265D, Beverly, MA 01915, USA.

ISBN: 978-0-7858-4302-3

Publisher: Wendy Friedman
Senior Managing Editor: Meredith Mennitt
Senior Design Manager: Michael Caputo
Designer: Sue Boylan & Alana Ward
Editor: Cathy Davis
Image credits: Shutterstock